THE SWEDISH COOKBOOK

THE SWEDISH COOKBOOK

NIKLAS EKSTEDT

Photography by
Haarala Hamilton

BLOOMSBURY PUBLISHING
LONDON · OXFORD · NEW YORK · NEW DELHI · SYDNEY

Sweden has not always been a wealthy country. Our food culture was born out of scarcity, long winters, and the need to make the most of what little was at hand. Every recipe in this book carries echoes of those who came before: the home cooks who stretched ingredients with skill and patience, the mothers who turned hardship into nourishment, and the Swedish chefs who kept the flame alive through times of change.

This book is a tribute to that long struggle — and to the resilience that has shaped the flavours of Sweden.

CONTENTS

Introduction	10
Vegetables	**22**
Fish	**100**
Meat	**144**
Fika	**190**
Index	260
Thank You	266
About the Author	269

Introduction

I'm often asked what makes Swedish food different, and the simple answer is that Swedish food isn't just about eating, or taste, or specific ingredients; rather, it's about how we relate to food and how we bring it together. Swedish cooking is often simple, but with that simplicity comes a deep respect for the raw ingredients – we want to make them shine.

The flavours in Swedish food tend to be clean, sometimes tangy, often a little salty – and almost always seasonal. In fact, I love how our cuisine is rooted in nature and the seasons; how it comes simply, without trying to impress, from everything we have around us. Many dishes have a clear purpose: some food is made to last through winter, some to provide a quick meal after work, some intended as warm sustenance carried in a Thermos out into the woods. With all this in mind, Swedish food – even everyday food – has a thoughtful, humble quality. It feels honest.

The humility of Swedish food – a cuisine so often overlooked on the world stage – is exactly what speaks to me. I hope, over the following pages, it will speak to you too. Sharing my love for the food I grew up with, of my home, is exactly why I've written this book. When I became a chef, I realised there's a deep pride in Swedish food that we don't always talk about. I wanted to show that what we have here is worth celebrating – in restaurants, on TV and in this book – and it's that passion that drives me.

Introduction

The history and traditions of those who have cooked before us continue to shape how Swedes cook today. Many traditional techniques came out of necessity. Swedish winters are harsh, with temperatures hovering around freezing in the south, and dipping far below it in the north. Preserving food – through pickling, drying or fermenting – to see our ancestors through those brutally cold months was essential. Even though we don't *need* to preserve food in that way anymore, the Swedes I know (myself included) still love those flavours: the acidity, the fermentation, the smokiness. They are the flavours that have shaped our palates. They are also the flavours that we know will give way to the abundance of produce that comes in the spring. Then, as the season turns, we long for nettles and asparagus. Later in the year, in autumn, we yearn for mushrooms and game. Eating with the rhythm of the seasons is part of who we are.

I grew up with simple meals, and lots of potatoes, fish and creamy vegetables. But I am so thankful that my parents also encouraged me to eat broadly and to explore new tastes. While I imagine most people would say that Swedish food is known for its meatballs and cardamom buns – both of which are undoubtedly delicious (and unashamedly deserve a place in the book; see pages 169 and 257) – you'll also find recipes that go beyond to celebrate some of my favourite ingredients I've discovered along the way.

Introduction

Lingonberries and lingonberry jam (available in some supermarkets, or online; but use cranberries or cranberry sauce, if you can't find them), dill, cabbage, rye, wild game, herring, mushrooms… the list of Swedish staples goes on. When cooking with them, I like to highlight them in ways that never overcomplicates, that remains true somehow to the origins of the food I grew up with. A typical example – and a recipe that I care deeply about – is my recipe for cabbage rolls (see page 155). Even though I've played around with the flavours, the soul of the dish to this day reminds me of my grandmother. And then there's *gravad lax* (see page 110) – a dish that captures so much of what I love about Swedish food: it is fresh, slightly salty, beautiful and straightforward. To my mind, you don't need much more than that.

At my restaurants I'm known for using ancient Scandinavian cooking techniques. I cook with fire to make contemporary food with seasonal produce that showcases Swedish flavours. In the book, I've included some recipes that stay close to their origins, giving methods that are true to those used by the generations that came before us. Others, I have adapted. This is because, with reverence and respect for what has been, I want to show how you can cook Swedish food with what's in your kitchen now. Not to change it, but to keep it alive.

Introduction

So, is Swedish food easy to make at home? Undoubtedly, yes. You'll notice quickly that there tend to be few ingredients. The key is not to add more, necessarily, but to know how to treat what you do have well. In the book, I try to explain *why* we do things a certain way, and offer you tips and suggestions to make those ways *your* ways too. I don't want you necessarily just to follow instructions; I hope to have given you the building blocks to learn how each dish works; to enable you to try new flavours and dishes yourself in ways that make cooking – especially Swedish cooking – both easier and more rewarding.

A lot of the dishes in this book are perfect for our busy lives. For example, the Fried Pork with Onion Sauce, Corn and Sliced Apple on page 152, Cabbage Pudding with Kale and Lingonberries on page 176, Whole Roasted Arctic Char with Spinach, Broccoli, New Potato and Horseradish Salad on page 120 or Egg and Courgette Omelette with Tomato and Parsley Salad on page 33 are all delicious and quick to make at the end of the day.

Beyond these quick suppers, though, we Swedes are probably more well-known for our *smörgåsbords* – our buffet-style meals laden with traditional Swedish fare. They are a great way to feed a crowd, often featuring hot and cold dishes, made up of fish, potatoes, cheeses and eggs.

Introduction

The *smörgåsbord* is often a centrepiece of our celebrations: Midsummer, Christmas, Easter – each has its own typical dishes and flavours. There might be meatballs and *gravad lax* alongside pickled cucumber and crispbreads. The Swedish Anchovy and Potato Salad on page 134, Open Sandwiches on Rye Bread on page 225, Flatbread on page 216, Swedish Cheese Pie on page 222, Potato and Swedish Anchovy Gratin on page 137 and Swedish Dumplings with Meat Filling on page 163 are all recipes that speak to me of celebratory feasts. If you want to create your own *smörgåsbord*, don't hold back – pick your favourite recipes and invite a crowd.

I've tried to create a book that reflects how we *think about* food in Sweden – and for that reason, we have chapters covering vegetables, fish, meat and *fika*. For us, vegetables aren't just side dishes but potentially a whole meal; fish is a staple; meat is used respectfully; and *fika* ... well, *fika* is a whole world of its own.

Far from being just about coffee and cake, *fika* is about pausing, connecting, breathing; it's a feeling, like a little pocket of calm in the day. In a sense the sweet treat, although obligatory, is secondary to the opportunity for relaxation and social connection. To create your own stage for mid-morning *fika* (or, if you prefer, to round off a meal), in this chapter you'll find a whole range of bun recipes – cardamom, vanilla, cinnamon, semlor, saffron – as well as cookies, cakes, chocolate slices, pancakes, waffles, biscuits, flatbreads, pies and tarts.

As I mentioned at the start, for Swedes, cooking is about how we relate to food; how it makes us feel. You'll no doubt have heard of *hygge* – the Danish word that embodies a feeling of cosy contentment through everyday pleasures. For Swedes, it's all about *lagom*. English offers no perfect translation, but in essence the word means 'just right'; not too much, not too little. This is a sense you can see reflected time and again in our food. We like balance – flavours that work together in harmony, that never overpower each other. *Lagom* also manifests in how we think about portions and ingredients – everything in balance. Literally translated, though, the word is a conflation of two others that, in fact, tell you everything you need to know about the way the Swedes think: *lag* (meaning 'team') and *om* (meaning 'the whole'). For us, then, when it comes to life and food, it's all about the whole team.

In that spirit, join me. Let's dig in and get cooking.

Niklas

VEGETAB

Vegetables

Vegetables might not be the first thing that comes to mind when talking about Nordic cuisine, but they play a central role, making them incredibly important. In Sweden, we jokingly ask, 'How was the summer? Oh, that day was nice.' Our growing season is short and intense – winters are deep, cold and dark, and when summer finally arrives, it's as if the whole country exhales and longs for chlorophyll-rich delicacies. We celebrate the first potatoes with great love, and Swedish asparagus often makes front-page news. And what would Midsummer be without delightful, sweet strawberries?

In the past, vegetable availability was limited – you had some cabbages, potatoes and, if you were lucky, maybe asparagus. We Swedes became experts in fermenting and pickling as a way to preserve veg when our growing season was so short. By contrast, today we import vegetables from all over the world and have an abundance year-round (but we still love our pickles and ferments!). In this chapter, however, I want to highlight and celebrate beautifully fresh, seasonal vegetables, just as my ancestors did, in Sweden, in the past.

Vegetables

Vegetables are especially close to my heart because my parents met at a vegetable stall. My mother worked at one vegetable counter and my father at another, both at Medborgarplatsen in Stockholm in the 1970s. That was more than 50 years ago, and I love listening to the stories they tell from that time. They were young, had no money, and lived on the vegetables they took home from the stalls. When they later had three boys who were always hungry, vegetables became an obvious part of our meals. They weren't just something you put on the side of the plate – they formed the foundations of many dishes. Maybe not because my parents loved vegetables from the start, but because it was what they had access to, and nothing could go to waste.

I am eternally grateful to my parents for this, because now I love vegetables. In spring and summer, I live on them almost exclusively. Often, a meal at our house can be something as simple as freshly boiled new potatoes with lots of chopped dill, some capers and some browned butter. Another favourite in Nordic cuisine is cabbage. Today, there are many different varieties of cabbage, which makes me happy – pointed cabbage, kohlrabi and red cabbage are fantastic variations. Sure, it can get monotonous if you're reaching for just white cabbage, but with so many varieties available, you can really mix it up. There is an abundance of recipes in this chapter that showcase this humble veg.

So, with inspiration taken directly from my parents' kitchen table, it makes me so happy to share some of my favourite vegetable recipes with you. I hope you enjoy them as much as I did as a child, and I do to this day.

— ROMANSALLAT MED DILL OCH KRUTONGER —

Romaine Salad with Dill and Croûtons

Growing Romaine lettuce has become increasingly popular in Sweden in recent years, and it's easy to see why. It has a wonderfully crisp texture and a mild, nutty flavour, making it perfect for salads or as a fresh side dish to both hot and cold meals. In Swedish cuisine, we've always had a love for crisp, simple salads – just think of classic pizza salad (see page 30) or our fondness for dill and crunchy croûtons. This version makes the most of that penchant for dill and croûtons – it is a simple yet flavourful way to highlight the potential of Romaine leaves, and it pairs just as well with a piece of grilled fish as with a hearty dinner of meat and sauce.

SERVES 4

2 heads of Romaine lettuce, leaves separated
½ cucumber, sliced lengthways
3 tablespoons olive oil (optional, to make the croûtons)
2 slices of white bread, cut into about 1cm cubes (or use ready-made croûtons)
15g dill, torn or chopped
salt and black pepper
shavings of Västerbotten cheese, to serve (optional)

Tear the lettuce leaves into smaller pieces and place them in a salad bowl. Toss through the cucumber slices, then set aside.

If you're making your croûtons, heat the oil in a frying pan over a medium heat. Add the cubes of bread, and fry for 4 minutes, turning regularly, until golden and crispy all over. Scoop out the croûtons and place them on kitchen paper to drain the excess oil.

Sprinkle the torn dill over the lettuce leaves in the bowl and toss, then scatter over the croûtons. Season with salt and pepper, and finish with Västerbotten shavings to serve, if you wish.

TIP

For extra flavour, you can dress the salad with a simple vinaigrette of lemon and olive oil in a ratio of one-third lemon to two-thirds oil.

— VITKÅLSSALLAD MED BLÅBÄR OCH FRYST FETAOST —
Cabbage Salad with Blueberries and Shaved Frozen Feta

'Pizza salad', as this dish is sometimes known, is one of those simple yet genius combinations embedded in Swedish food culture. First served in pizzerias in the 1970s, it was inspired by tangy cabbage salads from the Balkans and Italy. Since then, though, it has evolved into something entirely unique; as a form of coleslaw. This version is one of my favourites (I always have a variation on the menu) – with feta cheese and blueberries, where the saltiness of the cheese meets the natural sweetness of the berries, and the tangy dressing ties everything together. It's fresh, adaptable and keeps well for days.

SERVES 4

300g white cabbage, cored and shredded
1 tablespoon olive oil
1 tablespoon lemon juice
100g blueberries (or use frozen, defrosted)
100g feta cheese, frozen
salt and black pepper

Tip the shredded cabbage into a salad bowl and pour over the olive oil and lemon juice. Gently turn the cabbage to coat it in the dressing. Scatter over the blueberries, grate over the frozen feta, then season with salt and pepper and serve.

TIP

You can swap the blueberries for raspberries or blackberries, if you prefer.

— ZUCCHINIOMELETT MED TOMAT- OCH PERSILJESALLAD —

Egg and Courgette Omelette with Tomato and Parsley Salad

Courgettes give this omelette a juicy texture – the result is simple, yet flavourful; and rustic, nourishing and easy to adapt to the seasons. In short, it captures the essence of traditional Swedish comfort food. The tomato salad adds acidity and balance, making this dish perfect as a light lunch or a quick dinner, ideally with a slice of good bread on the side.

SERVES 4

2 tablespoons sunflower oil
1 onion, chopped
1 courgette, sliced
a handful of cooked new potatoes, halved or quartered (optional)
4 eggs
a small bunch of thin asparagus, chopped into 3–4cm pieces (optional)
2 tomatoes, roughly chopped
1–2 small shallots, very finely chopped
a handful of flat-leaf parsley, leaves picked
1 tablespoon olive oil
salt and black pepper

Heat the oil in a 30cm frying pan over a medium heat. Reduce the heat to low and add the onion and courgette. Fry for 4–5 minutes, then add the cooked potatoes and fry for another 2–3 minutes, until the courgette has softened, the potatoes are warmed through, and the onion is translucent.

Meanwhile, in a bowl, lightly beat the eggs with a pinch of salt and 2 tablespoons of water until combined. Pour the egg mixture over the vegetables in the pan, increase the heat to medium and leave the omelette to cook for about 12 minutes, until slightly golden.

While the omelette is cooking, bring a saucepan of salted water to the boil. Add the asparagus, if using, and blanch for 1–2 minutes until only just tender. Drain and leave to cool until warm.

Mix the tomatoes in a bowl with the shallots, parsley and olive oil and season with salt and pepper. If using, stir through the warm asparagus.

Serve the omelette with the salad alongside.

TIP

Chopped fresh basil – in either the omelette or the salad – is a great way to further boost the sense of springtime in this dish.

GURKSALLAD MED GRODDAD SÖTMANDEL OCH SUMAK

Cucumber and Sprouted Almond Salad with Sumac

Soaking almonds in cold water overnight can enhance their flavour, reducing their natural bitterness to give them a fresh, light flavour. Like this, they are brilliant in all sorts of dishes – including this simple, bright cucumber salad.

SERVES 4

2 cucumbers, sliced
60g sprouted almonds
1 tablespoon olive oil
1 tablespoon lemon juice
1 teaspoon sumac

Place the cucumber slices in a salad bowl or serving dish and sprinkle them with the sprouted almonds.

Mix together the olive oil and lemon juice in a small jug, then pour the dressing over the salad.

Sprinkle with the sumac to serve.

— RÖDKÅLSSALLAD MED KAPRIS OCH CITRONSKAL —
Shredded Red Cabbage Salad with Capers and Lemon Zest

Red cabbage is one of those ingredients often associated with slow-cooked dishes and winter food, but it's also fantastic in fresh, crisp salads. Here, it gets the lively addition of lemon zest and capers, which highlight its natural sweetness and create a nice balance between acidity and saltiness. It's a salad that gets better after it's had a few hours to meld in the fridge and works wonderfully with both grilled fish and meat – or as a vibrant dish on its own.

SERVES 4

300g red cabbage, thinly shredded
2 tablespoons small capers, drained
pared zest of 1 lemon
1 tablespoon olive oil
salt and black pepper

Tip all the ingredients into a salad bowl and mix them together to combine. Season with salt and pepper and mix again to serve.

TIP

Add a little honey to balance the lemon's acidity, if you need.

— ÄRTSOPPA OCH PANNKAKOR —

Split Pea Soup with Pork
(followed by Pancakes with Lingonberry Jam and Cream)

People in Sweden have eaten pea soup with pork on Thursdays since the Middle Ages – Friday was a fasting day, so Thursday mealtimes were hearty and filling. In that vein, they were always followed by pancakes. While Swedes no longer observe fasting on Fridays, the tradition of having a soulful meal of peas and pork, finished with pancakes for dessert, lives on, especially in schools and the military.

SERVES 5–6

FOR THE SOUP
500g dried yellow split peas, soaked overnight (at least 12 hours)
2 onions, chopped
1 large carrot, peeled and sliced
1 teaspoon dried thyme
1 teaspoon dried marjoram (optional)
1 bay leaf (optional)
300g salted pork or ham (optional), cut into 2cm cubes
salt and black pepper

FOR THE PANCAKES
3 eggs
600ml whole milk
180g plain flour
½ teaspoon salt
3 tablespoons butter or oil
lingonberry jam and whipped cream, to serve

First, make the soup. Drain and rinse the split peas and place them in a large saucepan. Cover with 2 litres of water and place the pan over a high heat. Bring the water to the boil, skimming off any scum that rises to the surface. Once the water is boiling, add the onions, carrot, thyme, marjoram and bay leaf (if using), reduce the heat and simmer for about 1½–2 hours, until the split peas are soft. Add the pork or ham, if using, and cook for 30 minutes more. Season with salt and pepper.

While your soup is cooking, make the pancake batter. Combine the eggs and milk in a mixing bowl and add the flour and salt. Beat to a smooth batter, then set aside until you've eaten the soup!

To enjoy your dessert of pancakes, heat a little of the butter or oil in a frying pan over a medium heat. Once melted and hot, add a ladleful of the batter and swirl it around the pan to coat. Fry the pancake for about 2 minutes on each side until golden brown all over. Keep each pancake warm while you fry the remainder, adding oil or butter as needed.

Serve the pancakes with lingonberry jam and whipped cream, as a dessert to the soup (of course, you can have them any time without the soup, too!). This is a classic Swedish way to eat pea soup and pancakes. Enjoy!

Vegetables

— SMÖRSTEKT POTATIS MED KAPRIS OCH DILL —

Cubed New Potatoes Fried in Clarified Butter with Capers and Dill

I like to think of this dish as a modern twist on traditional Swedish *råraka* – crispy fried grated potatoes (not to be confused with Swedish *rösti*, which pre-cooks the potato before grating). Here, I'm cubing the potatoes, rather than grating them, then parboiling, and frying in clarified butter, which adds extra crispness and a nutty flavour. Served with tangy capers and fresh dill, it becomes a wonderfully balanced dish – perfect with a dollop of soured cream and vendace roe, or as a crispy side to fish and meat.

SERVES 4

800g Charlotte or Amandine potatoes, quartered
3 tablespoons clarified butter (or ghee), plus optional extra (melted) to serve
2 tablespoons small capers, drained
5g dill, finely chopped
a small handful of watercress
2–3 thyme sprigs, leaves picked
1 tablespoon white wine vinegar or lemon juice

TIP

Add a sprinkling of finely chopped red onion, or some lemon zest grated over the finished dish adds a bit of complementary freshness.

Bring a large saucepan of salted water to the boil. Add the potatoes and boil them for 5–8 minutes, until they will yield to being pressed with a spoon (but don't mash). Drain the potatoes and leave to steam dry in the colander for 10 minutes.

Heat a large frying pan over a medium heat and add the clarified butter. When hot, tip in the potatoes and fry them for 4–5 minutes, turning regularly, until golden and crispy all over. Tip the potatoes into a serving bowl and add the capers (or, if you prefer, you can fry the capers in the empty pan first, to make them crispy, too).

Add the dill, watercress and thyme to the bowl and drizzle with the vinegar or lemon juice, and extra clarified butter, if you like, just before serving.

HOW TO CLARIFY BUTTER

Place the butter in a pan over a low heat – as low as possible (on a scale of 1 to 10, opt for 1). Eventually, the butter will melt and, after a while longer, you'll notice that the milk proteins sink to the bottom of the pan and the clear part of the butter is on top – how long this takes will depend on how much butter you're clarifying. Carefully pour the clarified butter into a separate container, leaving the white residue in the pan (discard this). Refrigerate and use as needed.

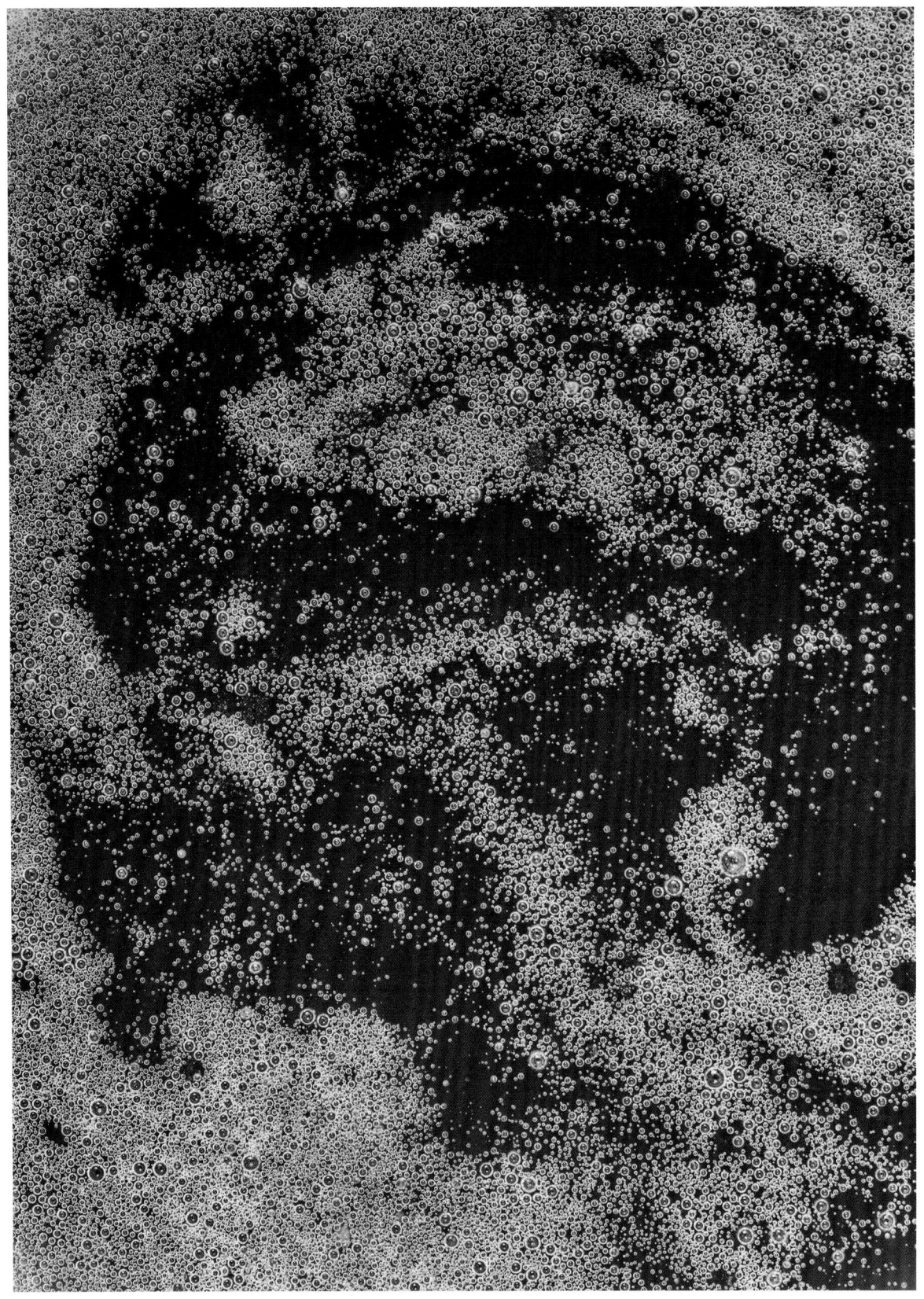

— GRILLAD SPETSKÅL MED CITRONSMÖR —
Grilled Pointed Cabbage with Lemon Butter

Pointed cabbage is one of the most rewarding vegetables to grill. Naturally mild in flavour, once it has wonderfully charred edges, it develops extra depth that gives it sweetness and a juicy texture. Simple yet tangy lemon butter brings a touch of sour. This is a versatile side dish, equally at home with fish, meat and vegetarian meals; or a light main if served topped with toasted nuts and a dollop of crème fraîche.

SERVES 4

1 pointed cabbage
50g butter, at room temperature; plus more (melted) for brushing
pared zest of 1 lemon
salt
a few mint leaves, sliced, to serve (optional)

Heat a barbecue or griddle until hot – if you hover your hand over the heated grill, you should need to move it after 5 seconds or so.

Cut the cabbage into four large wedges (or into six if it's particularly big) and place the wedges directly on the grill plate. Grill the wedges for 2–3 minutes on each side, brushing regularly with butter, until nicely charred all over. Don't worry if the outer leaves get burnt; you can peel them off, or leave them for extra flavour.

Meanwhile, in a bowl mix together the 50g of softened butter and the lemon zest and season with salt.

When the cabbage wedges are ready, remove them to a plate and dot them all over with the lemon butter. Leave it to melt, then serve scattered with the mint leaves, if using.

TIP

Top the cabbage with toasted almonds for a crunchy touch.

— KRÄMIG POTATISSALLAD MED GRÖNKÅL, GURKA OCH RÄDISOR —
Creamy Potato Salad with Kale, Cucumber and Radishes

In Sweden, if there is a summer barbecue, a buffet or a celebration to be had, potato salad will be there – it is a staple of Swedish cuisine. The salad is always available to buy pre-made, often in its most traditional form with a heavy mayonnaise base. But homemade potato salad is something entirely different – fresher, creamier and full of vibrant flavours.

This version is lighter than the classic, with crème fraîche instead of mayonnaise, and with crispy kale, cucumber and radishes, which add both colour and texture. It is perfect as a side to grilled food or part of a summery lunch, or as a hearty dish on its own (with a piece of crispbread and aged cheese on the side). It is a flavourful blend of tradition and innovation – just as Swedish cooking should be.

SERVES 4

800g salad potatoes (or use 1.1kg cooked leftover potatoes), skin on
100g kale, tougher leaves sliced
100ml crème fraîche
1 tablespoon Dijon mustard
a small handful of chives, finely chopped
a handful of shelled broad beans, blanched and skinned or blanched peas (optional)
1 cucumber, thickly sliced
10 pea shoots
6 radishes, thickly sliced
salt

If using raw salad potatoes, bring a pan of salted water to the boil over a high heat. Add the potatoes and boil for 12–15 minutes, or until tender. Drain and leave to cool completely. You can halve them if they're on the large side.

While the potatoes are cooling, massage the kale with a sprinkle of salt, until it becomes flexible and tender.

Combine the crème fraîche and Dijon mustard in a bowl.

Tip the cooled potatoes into a salad bowl and add the mustard mixture. Stir to combine, then stir through the chives, and the broad beans or peas (if using).

In a separate bowl, stir together the cucumber, pea shoots and radishes. Serve the salad vegetables in a bowl with the potatoes and the kale on the side.

TIP

For a little bit of a sharpness and tang, I sometimes like to add capers to this salad, too.

— GRILLAD KÅLRABBI —

Grilled Kohlrabi

Kohlrabi is an underrated Swedish vegetable. When grilled, it develops a wonderful sweetness and a soft yet crisp texture. In this recipe, it makes the perfect side dish for both fish and meat, or a substantial vegetarian dish on its own served with a dollop of butter or a fresh herb oil. The result is simple, flavourful and an excellent way to showcase this humble Nordic vegetable.

SERVES 4

3 kohlrabi, whole, skin on
2 tablespoons olive oil
salt and black pepper

Heat your grill to its highest setting. Place the kohlrabi on the grill pan and grill them for 30 minutes to 1 hour, turning regularly, until charred and blackened all over (the timing will depend on size).

Remove the kohlrabi from the grill and leave them to cool. Once cooled, cut them into smaller pieces (about 2–3cm) and serve drizzled with olive oil and seasoned with salt and pepper.

TIP

Drizzle the finished kohlrabi with honey for a sweeter touch.

— FÄNKÅLS- OCH APELSINSALLAD MED DILL OCH TRANBÄR —
Fennel and Orange Salad with Dill

This dish is usually served alongside fish, whether smoked or cooked. Its simplicity leaves the natural aniseed flavours of the fennel and dill to sing, and the orange to bring brightness. If apples are in season, they make a great alternative to oranges.

SERVES 4

1 large fennel bulb, trimmed
2 oranges, peeled
1 tablespoon white wine vinegar
2 tablespoons cold-pressed rapeseed oil (or light olive oil)
2 tablespoons finely chopped dill, plus fronds to serve
flaky salt and white pepper
2–3 tablespoons dried cranberries, to serve

Finely shave the fennel into thin slices – using a mandoline, if possible. Place the slices into a large salad bowl.

Segment the oranges and cut the segments in half. Add these to the bowl with the fennel, then drizzle over the vinegar and oil and lightly toss everything together to coat the ingredients in the dressing. Stir through the dill and season lightly with flaky salt and white pepper.

Serve cold as a side dish to fish, or on its own as a light lunch, with a few extra dill fronds and the dried cranberries scattered over.

— HELGRILLAD KÅLROT MED SALVIA —
Whole Roasted Swede with Sage

Swede is the English name for what elsewhere is called rutabaga. The literal translation of the Swedish *kålrot*, though, is 'cabbage root'. Whatever you call it, the vegetable was probably developed in Switzerland as a cross between a cabbage and a turnip. Regardless, it turned out to be very well suited to our northern climate.

SERVES 4

1 large swede, skin on
2 tablespoons olive oil
a few sage leaves (toast them very briefly in a pan with a little butter, if you wish)
a few thyme sprigs
salt and black pepper
lemon wedges, to serve

Heat your oven to 220°C/200°C fan.

Place the swede in a roasting tin and roast it for 1 hour, until soft. Test for doneness by inserting a skewer – if the skewer goes through easily, the swede is done. If not, pop it back in the oven and test again after another 10 minutes.

Once the swede is cool enough to handle, peel away the flaky, charred layer and slice the flesh into 2cm-thick pieces. Brush the slices with olive oil, and sprinkle over the sage leaves and picked thyme sprigs. Season with salt and pepper.

TIP

Add a little chopped garlic to the olive oil to make the dish more aromatic and savoury.

— SALLAD MED HALLON, ZUCCHINI OCH RÄDISOR —

Salad with Raspberries, Courgette and Chives

Raspberries are not only great for puddings, they're amazing as a side dish for both meat and fish. I use them a lot, especially at the beginning of the raspberry season when they're not so sweet. They taste fantastic with just about anything.

SERVES 4

2 handfuls of mixed salad greens (such as rocket, spinach or baby kale)
1 small courgette, thinly sliced
4–5 radishes, thinly sliced
150g raspberries
1 tablespoon olive oil
1 teaspoon lemon juice or apple cider vinegar
½ teaspoon runny honey (optional)
salt
2 tablespoons finely chopped chives, to garnish

In a large bowl, toss the mixed greens with the courgette and radishes, then scatter the raspberries over the top.

In a small bowl, to make the dressing, whisk together the olive oil, lemon juice or vinegar and honey (if using) and season with salt.

Drizzle the dressing over the salad and gently toss to combine. Then, sprinkle over the chopped chives to garnish.

— RAGGMUNK MED LINGON OCH GRÄDDFIL —

Potato Pancakes with Lingonberries and Soured Cream

Potato dishes are a staple in many countries, each with their twist or preferred methods of cooking. In Sweden, the beloved potato pancake, known as *raggmunk*, stands out as a favourite among young and old alike. Deeply rooted in Swedish culinary tradition, this simple and flavourful recipe is nostalgia in a potato dish: so many Swedes remember enjoying it as children, especially in school cafeterias.

SERVES 4

700g potatoes, peeled
1 small egg
2 tablespoons plain flour
a pinch of salt
butter or oil, for frying

FOR THE TOPPING
soured cream
lingonberries (defrosted if frozen)

Coarsely grate the potatoes and place them in a sieve. Press down firmly with a clean tea towel to squeeze out as much liquid as possible.

Tip the potatoes in to a clean, dry mixing bowl and add the egg, flour and salt. Stir to combine.

Heat the butter or oil in a frying pan over a medium heat. When hot, take one quarter of the mixture and add it to the pan, pressing it down with the back of a spatula into a thin pancake shape. Fry the potato pancake for 2–3 minutes, until the underside is golden and crisp, then flip it over and fry for another 2–3 minutes, until cooked through. Repeat for the remaining mixture, until you have 4 pancakes altogether.

Serve immediately with soured cream and lingonberries on top.

TIP

Your favourite roe, chopped chives and finely chopped red onion make a great, savoury alternative to top these potato pancakes.

— SALLAD MED BÖNOR, LINSER OCH MYNTA —

Broad Beans with Mint Salad

I love how the right flavour combinations can make simple dishes feel luxurious. This salad with broad beans and mint is exactly that – just a few ingredients, yet full of freshness and texture. I love serving it alongside grilled food, as a light starter or simply on its own with a piece of good bread. Simple, green and always appreciated.

SERVES 4

200g green beans (such as haricots verts or wax beans)
200g shelled broad beans
100g mint, leaves picked (chopped if you wish)
3 tablespoons olive oil
1 tablespoon lemon juice

Bring a saucepan of lightly salted water to the boil over a high heat. Add the green beans and shelled broad beans and blanch them briefly for 1–2 minutes, to just take the edge off the rawness. Drain, then when cool enough to handle, chop them into 1cm lengths.

In a bowl, mix together the broad and green beans and the mint. Add the olive oil and lemon juice and toss everything together to combine.

TIP

A sprinkling of grated parmesan brings a touch of saltiness that pairs so well with the fresh beans and mint.

— STEKT SVAMP MED GRÖNA ÄRTER OCH BRÄND GRÄDDE —
Fried Mushrooms with Peas and Burnt Cream

I created this dish through my own happy accident. I love eating fried mushrooms, especially with a simple sauce. Intending to make a white wine and cream sauce, I left the pan too long and burnt the contents a little. The result, though, was fantastic and, like so many recipes from history, it felt like an accident turned stroke of genius! Since then, I've made the dish many times and the secret is to keep whisking the cream until it starts to caramelise and smells slightly burnt. That's when it's ready.

SERVES 4

1 tablespoon butter
1 small onion, chopped
400g mushrooms of choice (I usually use chanterelles, but any mushrooms work well), cleaned but left whole
300ml double cream
200g frozen peas
salt and black pepper

FOR THE PARSLEY AND THYME SALAD
a handful of flat-leaf parsley, leaves picked and roughly chopped
4 thyme sprigs, leaves picked
1 tablespoon Dijon mustard
juice of 1 lemon
1 teaspoon runny honey
50ml olive oil

First, make the salad. Mix the parsley, thyme, mustard, lemon juice and honey in a bowl. Slowly whisk in the olive oil until the dressing emulsifies, then season with salt and pepper to taste. Set aside while you make the mushrooms and burnt cream.

Melt the butter in a frying pan over a medium heat. Add the onion and mushrooms, frying and turning occasionally, until the liquid they release has evaporated and the mushrooms are golden brown and cooked through (the precise time will depend on your choice of mushrooms).

Meanwhile, pour the cream into a saucepan and place it over a medium heat. Whisking continuously, bring the cream to a simmer and keep whisking until it begins to thicken (this will take a few minutes). Keep whisking until it thickens so as to almost burn – that's when you know it's done.

Add the peas to the cooked mushrooms, then cook for an additional 3 minutes, until the peas are tender, then season with salt and pepper.

Divide the mushrooms and peas between 4 serving plates and serve with a spoonful of the burnt cream on the side. Finish with a portion of salad.

Vegetables

— MARINERAD ZUCCHINI MED BLOMMOR OCH MYNTA —
Marinated Courgettes with Flowers and Mint

Over the years, I've experimented with countless courgette recipes, and I think the best way to enjoy this versatile vegetable is by simply marinating the ribbons in a touch of lemon juice and seasoning. Although this is not a traditional Swedish dish, it has become a favourite in Sweden because courgettes are easy to grow here and adaptable to prepare. People in this part of the world seem to love them. I grow courgettes in the garden and, in season, I often find myself with an abundance of them.

SERVES 4

- 2 courgettes, thinly sliced into ribbons
- 1 tablespoon olive oil
- 1 tablespoon lemon juice
- 2 tablespoons finely sliced mint leaves
- 1 tablespoon chopped chives (optional)
- 2 tablespoons chopped flat-leaf parsley leaves (optional)
- 2 courgette flowers, torn

Tip the courgettes into a bowl and pour over the olive oil and lemon juice. Toss the courgettes to coat, and leave them to marinate for 30 minutes.

Sprinkle over the mint leaves, and the chives and parsley (if using), then scatter over the courgette flowers and serve.

TIP

Swap courgette flowers for other edible flowers, such as nasturtiums or marigolds, if you wish.

— RABARBERKOMPOTT MED YOGHURT —
Rhubarb Compôte with Yoghurt

When I was young, in summer we would pick rhubarb straight from the garden, dip it in sugar and eat it raw. This compôte is a grown-up version of that memory – still tart and fresh, but balanced by the sweetness of a handful of strawberries and a spoonful of creamy yoghurt in the serving. The combination may be simple but it never disappoints and it has a quiet confidence that is somehow very Swedish.

SERVES 4

500g rhubarb, peeled and cut into 2–3cm pieces
100g strawberries, hulled
100g caster sugar
pared zest and juice of 1 lemon
1 teaspoon vanilla sugar
natural yoghurt, to serve

Place the rhubarb, strawberries, caster sugar and lemon zest and juice in a saucepan over a medium heat. Leave the sugar to dissolve and the rhubarb to release its juice, then bring the liquid to the boil. Reduce the heat and simmer for 10–15 minutes, until the fruit is soft.

Remove the pan from the heat and stir in the vanilla sugar. Leave the compôte to cool and serve it spooned over bowlfuls of yoghurt. The compôte will keep in a sterilised, airtight jar in the fridge for up to 2 weeks.

BLOMKÅLSSOPPA MED ROSTADE SOLROSKÄRNOR
Cauliflower Soup with Roasted Sunflower Seeds

I always have a soup on the lunch menu in my brasserie restaurant, and it is always seasonal. It's fun to see how guests react to the different flavours we present for them. I think cauliflower would probably be the soup that people enjoy the most. That happy reaction, though, seems at odds with a general trend: it seems to me that lately we have stopped using cauliflower in everyday cooking. When I was a kid, we had cauliflower at least once a week. This soup is my start of a cauliflower revival.

SERVES 4

1 litre vegetable stock
1 cauliflower, broken into florets, reserve a few and the leaves for garnish
1 onion, chopped
50g sunflower seeds
100ml single cream
1 tablespoon small capers, to garnish
a few Romanesco cauliflower florets, sliced, to garnish (optional)
olive oil, for drizzling

Pour the stock into a medium saucepan and place it over a high heat. Once boiling, add the cauliflower and onion and boil for about 10 minutes, or until soft.

Meanwhile, heat a dry frying pan over a medium heat and add the sunflower seeds. Toast for 5 minutes, shaking the pan from time to time, until they are golden and fragrant. Immediately remove them to a plate so that they don't burn.

When the vegetables are ready, remove the soup pan from the heat and, using a hand-held blender, blitz until smooth. Stir in the cream and return the pan to the heat to heat through to piping hot.

Serve the soup in bowls sprinkled with the sunflower seeds and garnished with the reserved cauliflower florets and leaves, the capers, and the Romanesco florets, if using. Finish with a drizzle of olive oil.

TIP

A pinch of grated nutmeg sprinkled into the soup when you stir in the cream adds a layer of warming, gentle spice.

UGNSROSTADE RÖDBETOR MED GURKA OCH KRONDILL
Baked Beetroot with Cucumber Ribbons and Crown Dill

Baking is truly one of the simplest and most foolproof ways to prepare beetroot. Just pop the beetroots in the oven and let them roast beautifully alongside whatever else you might be cooking – whether it be chicken, pork or even a pie. During baking, beetroots develop a lovely, tender texture. They are perfect served warm, dotted with cold butter and with an ice-cold beer on the side.

SERVES 4

4 beetroots
1 cucumber, thinly sliced into ribbons
5g crown dill (the flowering heads of dill; or use regular dill, if unavailable), picked
1 tablespoon olive oil

Heat the oven to 220°C/200°C fan.

Pop the beetroots into a roasting tin and roast them in the oven for 45 minutes, until soft. Remove them from the oven and, once cool enough to handle, peel them and chop them into large chunks. Place the chunks in a serving dish.

Arrange the cucumber ribbons over the beetroots, then sprinkle with the picked crown dill and drizzle with the olive oil to serve.

TIP

Add some crumbled goat's cheese to the salad to give it a creamier texture and a sharp, tangy flavour.

— PUMPA-OCH SAFFRANSSUFFLÉ —
Pumpkin and Saffron Soufflé

We always serve a dessert soufflé at the restaurant. In autumn, when pumpkin season comes, I like to make this version. Getting it to rise as high as a traditional vanilla soufflé is a tricky business, but that doesn't matter too much: this method yields a slightly lower rise than vanilla versions, but remains incredibly creamy and totally delicious.

SERVES 4

- butter, for greasing
- 2 tablespoons caster sugar, plus a little extra for the ramekins
- about 100g smooth pumpkin purée (see page 78 for homemade, or use the purée from a babyfood jar)
- 0.5g saffron
- 3 egg whites
- whipped cream or crème fraîche, to serve

Heat the oven to 240°C/220°C fan. Butter the insides of four small ovenproof ramekins and lightly dust them with sugar (this helps the soufflé to rise).

In a bowl, mix the pumpkin purée with the saffron. Let it sit for a while (just while you whisk the whites in the next step should do it) so the saffron can infuse the purée.

Meanwhile, in a clean mixing bowl whisk the egg whites to stiff peaks. A little at a time, add the 2 tablespoons of sugar, continuing to whisk until the meringue is glossy and stiff.

Using a spatula, gently fold the pumpkin-saffron mixture into the meringue until no streaks remain, but taking care not to over-mix and risk knocking out the air.

Spoon the mixture equally into the ramekins, filling each to the top. Run a finger around the rim of each ramekin to make sure it's clear, which will help the soufflé rise evenly.

Place the soufflés on a baking sheet and transfer them to the centre of the oven. Bake for about 5 minutes, until they have risen beautifully and the tops are lightly golden.

Serve immediately, ideally with lightly whipped cream or a dollop of crème fraîche to balance the sweetness.

...continued overleaf

Roasted Pumpkin Purée

Heat the oven to 200°C/180°C fan.

Cut the pumpkin in half and scoop out the seeds. Slice the pumpkin into medium-sized wedges or chunks, leaving the skin on – this helps hold everything together while roasting. Place the pumpkin pieces on a baking tray. Drizzle with olive oil and sprinkle over a little salt. Roast for around 50–60 minutes, or until the flesh is soft and caramelised at the edges. The exact timing will depend on the size of your pumpkin pieces and the variety of pumpkin.

Once cooked, remove the tray from the oven and allow the pumpkin to cool slightly. Scoop the soft flesh away from the skin and place it in a blender or food processor. Blend until completely smooth. If the purée is very thick, you can add a splash of water to loosen it slightly.

Use immediately or store it in the fridge for up to 3 days. It also freezes beautifully.

— SÖTA JORDGUBBAR MED BASILIKA OCH FRYST FETAOST —

Honey and Basil Marinated Strawberries with Frozen Feta

The key to this dish is to use good-quality honey, adjusting the amount depending on how sweet the strawberries are: the riper the strawberries, the less honey you'll need. For balance, you could add a few drops of balsamic vinegar. Freeze the feta as long as possible before you begin, ideally putting it in the freezer the day before you intend to serve. Use a chilled grater for the best results. The contrast between room-temperature strawberries, sweet honey and salty frozen feta is incredible. The dish makes for a quick starter or side dish – I've made it many times when I'm hosting a barbecue at home.

SERVES 4

500g strawberries
2 tablespoons runny honey
about 4 basil sprigs, whole or leaves picked and finely sliced as you prefer
balsamic vinegar, to taste (optional)
100g feta cheese, frozen

In a salad bowl, toss the strawberries with the honey and basil until evenly combined. Give it a taste and add a drop or two of balsamic vinegar for balance, if needed.

Grate over the frozen feta and serve immediately.

TIP

Swap the feta for frozen halloumi if you like things a little saltier.

— KLASSISK GRÖNSAKSSOPPA MED POTATIS —

Vegetable Stew with Potatoes, Romanesco, Golden Beetroots and Brussels Sprouts

At home, I make vegetable stew at least once a week, especially when the vegetables in the fridge start to soften. (I'm a master at buying too many vegetables.) The idea here is to simmer a lot of vegetables in one pot and serve it just so — anything that's languishing in the fridge is a contender. For a heartier dish, add some lentils.

SERVES 4

1 litre vegetable stock
400g any potatoes, peeled and chopped into bite-sized pieces
200g Romanesco cauliflower, broken into bite-sized pieces
200g golden beetroots, peeled and chopped into bite-sized pieces
200g Brussels sprouts, halved
salt and black pepper
1 apple, peeled, cored and thinly sliced, to garnish (optional)

Pour the stock into a medium saucepan and place it over a medium–high heat. Bring the liquid to the boil, then reduce the heat to a simmer and add the veg. Leave to simmer for about 20 minutes, or until everything is tender. Taste and season with salt and pepper, if necessary (seasoning will depend on the flavour of your stock).

Serve the soup in bowls, garnished with wafer-thin slices of apple if you wish.

TIP

Experiment by adding herbs for extra layers of flavour — thyme and flat-leaf parsley work especially well.

— **BLÅBÄRSSOPPA MED SAFFRANSSKORPOR OCH GRÄDDVIRVEL** —

Blueberry Soup with Saffron Rusks and a Splash of Cream

In Sweden, we often enjoy blueberry soup during winter, especially from flasks while also cross-country skiing! It's that memory that makes this a nostalgic dish for me – trips in the snow, flasks of warm soup on the way. For the best results, try to use wild frozen blueberries, which are much tastier than cultivated ones. I've added saffron rusks here. They're made using leftovers from saffron buns (see page 219), which I've sliced thinly and baked at 150°C/130°C fan until crisp – it's a great way to use up old buns or pastries.

SERVES 4

300g frozen blueberries, preferably wild
100g caster sugar
1 tablespoon lemon juice
100ml whipping cream
4 saffron rusks (see recipe introduction), to serve

Pour 100ml of water into a medium saucepan. Add the blueberries, sugar and lemon juice and place the pan over a high heat. Bring the liquid to the boil, then simmer for 10 minutes, until the blueberries have broken down.

Meanwhile, whip the cream to thicken it a little.

Using a hand-held blender, blitz the blueberry mixture until smooth (or your preferred texture). Serve it in bowls, each topped with a saffron rusk and a swirl of cream.

TIP

Substitute the blueberries with blackberries, if you prefer.

KOKTA VAXBÖNOR MED DILLSMÖR OCH ÄPPLE
Boiled Yellow Wax Beans with Dill Butter and Apple

A classic from the Nordic summer kitchen, yellow wax beans are always best served simply: boiled, with butter and salt, when they're in their prime. For me, they taste like late August and dinners in the garden.

SERVES 4

400g yellow wax beans (or use green beans)
50g butter, at room temperature
1 tablespoon finely chopped dill
1 apple, peeled, cored and finely sliced
salt

Bring a medium saucepan of salted water to the boil over a high heat. Add the beans and boil for 5–7 minutes, until tender. Drain, then rinse them under cold water and set aside. (You can do this up to 2 hours in advance – just re-heat the beans in a little oil and extra butter when you're ready, and continue with the recipe.)

Tip the beans into a serving dish.

Mix the room-temperature butter with the dill and a pinch of salt until evenly combined. Dot the butter over the beans, add the finely sliced apple and toss together to serve.

TIP

Add a splash of lemon juice to the apple slices to stop them browning, and to balance the butter's richness, if you like.

— SPARRIS MED HOLLANDAISESÅS OCH CAYENNEPEPPAR —
Hollandaise Sauce with Boiled Asparagus and Cayenne Pepper

Traditionally, in Sweden, boiled asparagus stems are served whole with a thick sauce. In this case, tangy Hollandaise is perfect for balancing the bittersweet vegetables. I've given two methods for making the Hollandaise (one traditional, and one with kitchen gadgetry to speed up the process a little), and I've stuck with boiling the asparagus, but I've sliced them (I like them in little mounds on the sauce). If you prefer, you could fry the whole or sliced asparagus in a bit of oil over a high heat. Frying preserves more of the chlorophyll, giving the finished dish a more vibrant green colour.

SERVES 4

2 egg yolks
1 tablespoon lemon juice
150g butter, melted
cayenne pepper, to taste, plus more to garnish
200g asparagus, trimmed and cut into 2cm pieces
salt

Make the hollandaise. Bring a large saucepan of water to the boil over a high heat. Reduce the heat to a simmer and place a heatproof mixing bowl in the rim of the pan. Make sure the base of the bowl is not touching the water.

Add the egg yolks and lemon juice to the bowl and whisk vigorously over the simmering water until they thicken. Then, little by very little, whisk in the melted butter until you have a thick, glossy emulsion. Whisk in a little cayenne pepper to taste. Remove the bowl from the heat and set aside.

Alternatively, make the hollandaise in a food processor or blender – once the yolks and lemon are whisked and thickened in the bowl of the processor, gradually add the butter through the feed tube, whisking constantly. Add the cayenne and a pinch of salt to taste in the same way.

Bring a pan of salted water to the boil and add the asparagus. Boil for 3–5 minutes (depending on thickness), until just tender, and then drain.

Spoon the hollandaise into a serving dish and scatter the asparagus over the top. Sprinkle with more cayenne to garnish.

SVARTRÖTTER MED HASSELNÖTS- OCH PERSILJEPESTO
Salsify with Hazelnut and Parsley Pesto

Available year-round, salsify was a common vegetable in the mid-90s when I started out in the Swedish restaurant industry. We called it 'poor man's asparagus'. Peeling salsify was tedious because it arrived covered in soil, but now that I've come to appreciate its unique flavour, I think it was worth the effort. You don't see it around so much any more, but perhaps it's time for us to spark a revival.

SERVES 4

400g salsify (or asparagus), trimmed
1 lemon, juiced (husk reserved)
100ml whole milk
salt

FOR THE HAZELNUT PESTO
50g hazelnuts, roughly chopped (fresh, if available)
100g flat-leaf parsley, leaves and tender stems picked and roughly chopped
100ml olive oil

Peel the salsify, rub it with the lemon husks, and place it (or the asparagus) in a bowl with the milk. Reserve 1 tablespoon of the lemon juice and add the remainder to the milk. Leave the vegetables to soak while you boil the water.

Bring a large saucepan of salted water to the boil over a high heat. Once the water is boiling, drain the salsify (or asparagus), discarding the milk mixture and the lemon husk, and add the salsify (or asparagus) to the pan. Boil the salsify for 10–15 minutes (or the asparagus for 5–7 minutes, depending on size), until tender.

Meanwhile, make the pesto. Crush the hazelnuts in a mortar with the parsley, olive oil and reserved lemon juice until coarse and combined.

Drain the vegetables and tip them into a serving bowl. Spoon over the pesto and toss to coat. Serve straightaway.

TIP

Replace the hazelnuts in the pesto with walnuts or almonds, if you prefer.

— JORDÄRTSKOCKSSOPPA MED FÄRSKA ÖRTER —

Jerusalem Artichoke Soup with Herbs

A favourite in many Scandinavian kitchens (certainly in mine) this is a smooth and subtle soup with a gentle, nutty flavour. The artichokes do most of the work – which is just as it should be.

SERVES 4

1 litre vegetable stock
500g Jerusalem artichokes, peeled
1 onion, quartered
100ml single cream
salt and black pepper
finely chopped fresh herbs, such as thyme and flat-leaf parsley, or your favourite herb oil, to garnish

Pour the vegetable stock into a saucepan over a high heat. Bring the liquid to the boil and add the artichokes and onion. Boil for 20 minutes, until tender.

Remove the pan from the heat and use a hand-held blender to blitz the soup until smooth. Then, stir in the cream. Return the pan to the heat and warm through. Taste and season with salt and pepper, if necessary (seasoning will depend on the flavour of your stock).

Serve the soup in bowls, garnished with your chosen herbs or a swirl of your favourite herb oil.

TIP

Add a little peeled garlic with the onions for extra savouriness.

— STEKT GRÖNKÅL MED MANDEL- OCH VITLÖKSVINÄGRETT —
Fried Kale with Grated Almond and Garlic Vinaigrette

The first time I visited a French restaurant actually in France, I was served a salad with both raw and cooked artichoke. It was the first time I'd seen the same ingredient in its uncooked and cooked states on one plate, and it was a revelation. Ever since, I've been experimenting with different vegetables prepared both ways, and kale works especially well. That's the idea behind this dish – crispy fried kale alongside soft, raw kale. Delicious.

SERVES 4

- 500g kale, tough stalks and ribs removed
- 2 tablespoons sunflower oil
- 2 teaspoons salt
- 50g flaked almonds (or grated blanched whole almonds)
- 1 garlic clove, crushed
- 2 tablespoons olive oil
- 1 tablespoon white wine vinegar
- 1 whole, blanched almond, finely grated, to serve (optional)

Weigh out 300g of the kale and set it aside.

In a large saucepan, heat the sunflower oil over a medium–high heat. Add the separated 300g of kale and fry it for 2 minutes, turning occasionally, until reduced and crispy – you should be left with 200g of fried kale. Set it aside to drain on kitchen paper.

Shred the remaining 200g of raw kale and tip it into a serving bowl with the 2 teaspoons of salt. Massage the salt into the shredded leaves and let it sit for 5 minutes so that the kale becomes tender.

Meanwhile combine the almonds, garlic, olive oil and vinegar in a bowl.

Tip the drained crispy kale into the bowl with the raw kale, and pour the dressing over the top. Toss to coat and combine, then serve with grated blanched almond over the top, if you wish.

TIP

Replacing almonds with walnuts will give the dish an interesting, gnarly texture – a great variation!

FISH

When I was little, the days at school when we had fish for lunch were always my favourite. Perhaps it wasn't every other child's favourite day, but I wasn't like every other child when it came to food. I loved everything – I ate everything, smelled everything, tasted everything. Fish was my absolute favourite. If it was a wedding, a birthday or some other celebration, cod was often on the menu (and, if we were lucky, maybe some shellfish too), so to me fish always represented something special or festive.

In Sweden, we have the fantastic advantage of having two seas on our coastline – the Baltic Sea and the North Sea – which gives us access to an incredible variety of fish and shellfish. Unfortunately, during my lifetime, the Baltic Sea has been severely affected by human activity; we have treated it as an endless resource without thinking about the consequences. Fish stocks have dwindled drastically, and, where we once had an abundance of different fish species, some have now almost disappeared. Herring and other pickled fish, which have been the backbone of Swedish cuisine for generations, now seem a remnant of a bygone era. Whereas I might have filled an entire book with Swedish herring recipes, I have chosen here to share just one (Pickled Fried Herring on page 109). Eating herring is intrinsic to our culinary history, so the recipe absolutely earns its place, but it is on my mind not to contribute to the depletion of our seas. We are caught in a perpetual balancing act.

Fish

I know many people may also feel hesitant about salmon. Although salmon is not always farmed sustainably, there are initiatives trying to change this. So, if we make sure to buy salmon only a few times a year, and from sustainable sources, I think we should feel happy to eat it with a clear conscience.

Fish, then, is something that requires conscious decision-making, and I want to encourage you to stay informed about what is happening in our seas and on the market. Navigating the complexities can feel difficult, but we all need to do what we can. For that reason, don't get too hung up on exactly which fish I use in these recipes. Instead, feel free to substitute with other species that may be more sustainable and available to you wherever you are. Remember that, at its heart, Swedish cooking is respectful of its ingredients – and cooking according to Swedish principles is as much what this book is about as rustling up Swedish food.

This chapter presents some of my favourite Swedish fish dishes. Often they are those that have a connection to our culinary culture – like *gravad lax* (see page 110). The word *gravad* is from the Swedish term for 'buried' and references the tradition of curing fish by covering it entirely with a mixture of salt, sugar and herbs. We use this technique, which has existed in Swedish kitchens for hundreds of years, not only for salmon but also for other types of fish. So, here are some fish recipes that I love – from *gravad lax* to cod with egg sauce. These dishes are full of history and flavours that (just as much as meatballs) represent the wonderful abundance of Swedish cuisine.

— TOAST SKAGEN MED FÄRSK CITRON —
Toast Skagen with Fresh Lemon

Among summer's most popular Swedish dishes, toast Skagen is – strangely – named after an area in Denmark… The story goes that the famous Swedish chef Tore Wretman was sailing near Denmark, on his way to Sweden, and quickly put together a lunch on the boat. Someone on the boat asked, 'Tore, what is this dish called?' He replied, 'It's called Skagen, of course,' and pointed towards the land. Today, it comes in all sorts of variations, but this is my favourite.

SERVES 4

300g cooked, peeled small prawns, coarsely chopped
100g mayonnaise
2 tablespoons finely chopped dill
4 slices of thick-cut white bread or brioche
1 lemon, cut into wedges
salt and black or white pepper

In a bowl, mix the prawns with the mayonnaise and dill and season with salt and pepper to taste.

Toast the bread until golden brown on both sides – either in a toaster or in a frying pan over a medium heat. Slice the toast into strips ('soldiers') and divide them between your serving plates.

Spoon the prawn mixture equally between the plates and finish each serving with a wedge of lemon for squeezing.

TIP

Add some finely grated lemon zest to the prawn mixture for extra freshness. For a more luxurious touch, try topping with a spoonful of roe.

— STEKT INLAGD STRÖMMING PÅ TORE WRETMANS VIS —

Pickled Fried Herring with Red Onion and Rye Bread 'Tore Wretman-style'

Tore Wretman made this recipe famous by merging traditional Swedish flavours with the classic technique of contrasting vinegar and sugar with fried fish. Here, the crispy, fried surface of the breaded herring balances the tangy and sweet softness of the pickles. While the dish requires some planning, the result is worth it. I also believe this recipe is one of the best Swedish recipes for anyone wanting to start pickling fish but feeling a bit unsure. Self-doubt is not unreasonable – pickling herring and sprats can be tricky and sometimes very time-consuming. However, this recipe is almost guaranteed to succeed. If you can't find herring or sprats, mackerel is a great substitute.

SERVES 4

1kg herring fillets or sprats, cleaned
60g rye flour
50g butter
salt and white pepper
rye bread and crème fraîche, to serve

FOR THE PICKLING LIQUID
200ml distilled white vinegar (12% acidity)
300g caster sugar
1 red onion, sliced
1 carrot, peeled and thinly sliced
10 white peppercorns
2 bay leaves

First, to make the pickling liquid, pour 400ml of water into a medium saucepan. Add the vinegar and sugar and place the pan over a medium heat. Bring the liquid to the boil and leave it to bubble away until the sugar has dissolved. Remove the pan from the heat. Add the onion, carrot, peppercorns and bay leaves and leave to cool completely before using.

Meanwhile, lightly season the herring fillets or sprats with salt and white pepper. Tip the rye flour into a shallow dish and dip the fish into it, coating them lightly on both sides.

Put the butter in a frying pan over a medium heat and leave it to melt and get hot. Once hot, fry the herring fillets or sprats until golden on both sides – about 2–3 minutes per side, depending on the size of the fish. Leave the fried fillets to cool slightly.

Using two 1-litre sterilised glass jars, in layers add the fried fish, and the pickled onions and carrots (simply pick the onions and carrots out of the cooled pickling liquid). When everything has been layered, pour the remaining cooled pickling liquid into the jars, until it completely covers the layers. Put the lid on each jar, and store them in the fridge for at least 24 hours, or preferably longer (up to 1 week), to allow the flavours to develop.

Serve the herrings on a buffet with slices of rye bread and spoonfuls of crème fraîche, or with boiled potatoes, crispbread and a dollop of butter. Pickled fried herring is also excellent as an open sandwich topping (see page 226).

— GRAVAD LAX —
Cured Salmon

Gravad lax (or gravlax as it is more commonly known in English) is one of the most iconic dishes in Swedish cuisine, with roots stretching back to the Middle Ages. In the past, salmon was salted, then buried in the ground to preserve it. In fact, the word *gravad* is derived from another Swedish word, *begravd*, literally meaning 'buried' (today we use *begravd* almost exclusively in relation to funerals). The technique for curing the fish has, of course, evolved since those early days, but the principle remains the same: to cure salmon carefully with sugar, salt and dill, then leave it to mature slowly to perfection. This recipe achieves a wonderful combination of salty, sweet and fresh.

MAKES 1 WHOLE FILLET

1kg salmon fillet, skin on
3 tablespoons salt
3 tablespoons caster sugar or light brown soft sugar
1 teaspoon black pepper
plenty of dill, torn
1 dried bay leaf, scrunched

Double check the salmon fillet for any bones — use tweezers to remove any you find and discard them.

Mix the salt, sugar and black pepper in a bowl. Rub the mixture over both sides of the salmon and place the fish in a plastic self-seal bag (and into a dish) or in a dish with the skin side down. Generously cover the salmon with dill and scatter over the scrunched bay leaf.

Seal up the bag, squeezing out any air, or tightly cover the fish with cling film. Place a weight on top to gently press the salmon downwards. Leave it to cure in the fridge for 48 hours, turning the salmon over halfway through.

Remove the salmon from the fridge and take it out of the bag or dish. Using a super-sharp knife on a board, slice the salmon thinly into wide strips. It will keep for up to 5 days, covered, in the fridge, or for up to 2 months in the freezer.

TIP

For a special twist, try adding a splash of Cognac or gin to the curing mixture.

— **GRAVAD LAX MED POCHERAT ÄGG OCH HOVMÄSTARSÅS** —
Gravad Lax with Poached Egg and Mustard Dill Sauce

In Sweden, *hovmästarsås* (mustard dill sauce) is the classic accompaniment to *gravad lax*. Mild yet distinctive, it is most often served during festival feasts such as at Christmas, Easter and Midsummer. For me, though, it has so much more versatility than simply being wheeled out at celebrations might suggest. I use it not only with cured fish, as here, but also with cold meats, roasted root vegetables or eggs, or on a hearty open sandwich with fried mushrooms or cold-smoked Arctic char or hot-smoked salmon.

SERVES 4

2 tablespoons distilled white vinegar (12% acidity)
4 eggs
300g *gravad lax* (see page 110), sliced
salt and black pepper
4 slices of thick, sourdough toast, to serve
a few dill fronds, to garnish (optional)

FOR THE SAUCE
2 tablespoons Swedish mustard
1 tablespoon Dijon mustard
1 tablespoon caster sugar
½ teaspoon salt
a pinch of black pepper, plus optional extra to season
1 tablespoon white wine vinegar
200ml sunflower oil
100g dill, finely chopped

First, make the sauce. In a bowl, whisk together both mustards with the sugar, salt, pepper and white wine vinegar.

Whisking vigorously, gradually add the oil – aim for a thin stream – until the sauce emulsifies and becomes thick and creamy. An electric whisk works well if you don't want to whisk by hand. Stir in the dill and season with more black pepper, if you like. This makes more sauce than you need for this recipe, but it tastes even better the day after making, and lasts in an airtight jar for up to a week in the fridge.

To assemble the dish, pour 1 litre of water into a medium saucepan. Add the white vinegar, put the pan over a medium heat, and bring the vinegary water to the boil. As soon as it's boiling, reduce the heat to a simmer.

Crack one of the eggs into a small bowl and slide it into the simmering water. Repeat for each egg – cooking 2 eggs at a time is best to maintain the water temperature. Poach the eggs for 3–4 minutes, until the whites are set but the yolks remain runny. Gently scoop the eggs from the water using a slotted spoon and set them aside on a plate lined with kitchen paper. Repeat for the remaining eggs.

Place a slice of toast on each serving plate. Divide the *gravad lax* equally between the 4 slices of toast. Serve with the poached eggs, garnished with a few extra dill fronds, if you wish, and a serving of mustard dill sauce on the side.

Fish

— TORSK MED PRESSAD POTATIS, ÄGGSÅS OCH RÖDLÖK —
Pan-fried Cod with Mashed Potatoes, Egg Sauce and Red Onion

Some dishes just feel right, no matter the occasion, and pan-fried cod with egg sauce is one of them. It's nothing complicated, nothing that requires obscure ingredients or hours in the kitchen – just clean, simple flavours that work together in perfect, natural harmony. I have always appreciated this kind of food. After long days in the restaurant kitchen, preparing ambitious dishes and experimenting with flavours for our guests, this is the kind of home-cooked meal I crave. Perfectly pan-fried cod, silky mashed potatoes, with a creamy egg sauce tying it all together – simple, and never boring.

SERVES 4

800g potatoes, peeled and cut into 4cm chunks
2 eggs
2 tablespoons butter, plus more for frying the cod
200ml whole milk
4 x 150g skinless cod fillets
1 red onion, finely chopped
a handful of chives, finely chopped
salt and black pepper

TIP

Add a little dill to the egg sauce for extra flavour, and serve with melted butter for added richness. A garnish of a little chopped hard-boiled egg is also nice.

Bring a large saucepan of salted water to the boil. Add the potatoes and boil for about 20 minutes, until soft (the precise time will depend on the size of your potato chunks). Add the eggs to the cooking water 8–10 minutes before the end of the potato cooking time, and cook until hard boiled. Remove the eggs from the water, submerge them immediately in cold water to stop the cooking process and leave them to cool while you mash the potatoes.

Drain the potatoes and leave them to steam dry for 10 minutes in the colander. Mash them through a potato ricer (ideally) back into the pan, or tip them back into the pan and use a potato masher. If you're using a ricer, you can either leave them 'riced' without combining to a smooth mixture, or beat them with a wooden spoon until completely smooth – it's up to you.

Peel the cooled eggs and finely chop them.

To make the egg sauce, melt the 2 tablespoons of butter in a small saucepan over a medium heat. Add the milk and stir in the chopped eggs. Let the sauce simmer for 1–2 minutes, until thickened and the eggs have dissolved into it. Set aside to keep warm.

Melt a little butter in a frying pan over a medium heat. Add the cod and fry for 4–5 minutes each side, until golden on the outside and cooked through. Season with salt and pepper.

To serve, place a piece of cod on to each serving plate. Add equal amounts of the egg sauce and a portion of potato. Sprinkle with red onion and chives to finish.

— HELSTEKT RÖDING MED FÄRSKPOTATIS OCH MYCKET GRÖNT —
Whole Roasted Arctic Char with Spinach, Broccoli, New Potato and Horseradish Salad

Arctic char has always been an absolute favourite fish for me. It's similar to salmon but more refined in both flavour and texture — almost like a hidden gem from our Nordic waters. To me, Arctic char is associated with trips to icy mountain streams and that special feeling of sitting by an open fire with a freshly cooked fish on my plate. In this recipe, I let the fish take centre stage.

SERVES 4

2 whole Arctic char (about 600g each), cleaned
4 lemon slices
a few dill fronds
50g butter, sliced
600g small new potatoes
200g longstem broccoli, chopped
200g frozen peas
100g fine green beans, trimmed
200g baby spinach
1 tablespoon grated horseradish
salt and black pepper

Heat the oven to 140°C/120°C fan.

Season the Arctic char with salt and pepper and score the skin on both sides. Open up each fish gently and place 2 slices of lemon inside each cavity along with a few fronds of dill. Close up the fish and place equal amounts of butter over the top. Place both fish into an ovenproof dish, then transfer the dish to the oven. Bake the fish for 30 minutes, until just cooked through.

Meanwhile, bring a large saucepan of salted water to the boil over a high heat. Add the potatoes and boil for 12–15 minutes, then add the broccoli, peas and beans and boil for 5 minutes more, until the potatoes are soft and the broccoli is tender but still has some bite.

Drain the potatoes, broccoli and peas together, tip them into a serving dish and stir through the spinach, leaving it to wilt in the residual heat of the other vegetables.

Serve the fish on top of the vegetables and sprinkle with grated horseradish to finish.

TIP

Add a lemon wedge when serving for extra freshness, or serve with browned butter for a nuttier, richer flavour. If you can't find Arctic char you can use salmon instead.

— RÖKT FISK MED ÄGG, PICKLAD RÖDLÖK OCH RIVEN PEPPARROT —

Smoked Fish with Soft-boiled Egg, Pickled Red Onion and Flatbread

In Sweden, we have a long tradition of pairing smoked fish with bread. Often, that means crispbread, but it might be even better with warm, soft flatbread. This dish is ideal for a summer lunch or light dinner. The combination of creamy lemon crème fraîche, tangy pickled onion, fresh greens, soft-boiled eggs and mild smoked fish is hard to beat. I use smoked mackerel here, but hot-smoked salmon works just as well. A grating of fresh horseradish adds brightness. You'll find the flatbread recipe on page 216.

SERVES 4

- 200ml crème fraîche or mayonnaise
- 1 tablespoon lemon juice, plus more if needed
- a pinch of salt, plus more to season
- 4 eggs
- 4 soft flatbreads (see page 216)
- 65g baby spinach or other leafy greens
- a few leftover boiled new potatoes (optional)
- 200–250g smoked mackerel (or use hot-smoked salmon), flaked into pieces
- 1 tablespoon grated horseradish

FOR THE PICKLED RED ONION
- 100ml distilled white vinegar (12% acidity)
- 200g caster sugar
- 1 large red onion, thinly sliced using a mandoline

First, make the pickled red onion. Pour the vinegar and sugar into a saucepan and add 300ml of water. Give it a stir and place it over a medium heat. Bring the liquid to the boil, then immediately remove the pan from the heat and add the onion. Leave it to sit for at least 30 minutes (the pickled onion will keep in the fridge for several days in an airtight container).

Meanwhile, mix the crème fraîche with the lemon juice and pinch of salt. Taste – it should be tangy and fresh, but adjust the salt and lemon if you need.

Boil the eggs in gently boiling water for 7–8 minutes, until they are soft-boiled. Immediately scoop the eggs into a bowl of iced water to stop the cooking process and cool them. Once the eggs are cool enough to handle, peel them and cut them in half.

Spread equal amounts of the crème fraîche over each flatbread. Add a generous handful of baby spinach on top, then distribute the potatoes (if using) and the smoked fish over the greens. Top with the egg halves and pickled onion, then scatter over the horseradish and serve.

— ÅNGKOKTA BLÅMUSSLOR MED ÄPPLE OCH DRAGON —
Steamed Mussels with Apples and Tarragon

Mussels might not be the first thing people associate with Sweden, but we have a long coastline, with the Baltic sea along our east coast, and a shore that nudges the North Sea, feeding into the North Atlantic Ocean, along the west. It's hardly surprising, then, that we have a strong tradition of cooking with what's available from our waters, and that means mussels, too. I've added apples and tarragon here, which give this dish a Nordic character, and reflect the seasonality that is so fundamental to how I try to cook.

SERVES 4

1kg live mussels
2 tablespoons butter
2 Cox apples, cored and sliced
200ml white wine
100ml single cream
1 tablespoon chopped tarragon leaves, plus a few whole leaves, to garnish
a few black peppercorns
white, crusty bread, to serve

Rinse the mussels thoroughly and discard any that do not close when they are tapped.

Melt the butter in a large saucepan (use one with a lid) over a medium–high heat. Add the apple slices and sauté for 2–3 minutes, until slightly softened. Add the wine, cream, tarragon and peppercorns.

Add the mussels, cover the pot, and cook over a medium heat for 5–7 minutes, or until the mussels have opened. Shake the pot occasionally. Discard any mussels that do not open.

Serve the mussels garnished with a few whole tarragon leaves, with the bread on the side to soak up the sauce.

TIP

For extra depth of flavour, add a little finely chopped shallot along with the apples.

— KLASSISK FISKGRATÄNG MED DILL OCH RÄKOR —
Fish and Cheesy Béchamel Gratin in a Potato Crown

If ever there were a modern take on a classic comfort food, this is it. It's a cheesy, buttery mashed potato ring, filled with fish and prawns in a creamy, cheesy sauce. It's the kind of food that warms you from the inside on even the coldest Scandinavian days.

SERVES 4

FOR THE MASHED POTATO
1kg floury potatoes (such as Maris Piper), peeled and cut into 4cm chunks
50g butter
100g mature cheddar cheese, grated
lemon juice, to taste
salt and white pepper
a splash of milk or single cream (optional)

FOR THE FILLING
2 tablespoons butter
2 tablespoons plain flour
400ml whole milk
100g mature cheddar cheese, grated
a pinch of nutmeg (optional)
300g white fish fillets (such as cod or coley), cut into chunks
150g cooked, peeled small prawns
finely chopped dill, to garnish (optional)

Bring a saucepan of salted water to the boil and add the potatoes. Boil over a high heat for 15–20 minutes, or until soft (the precise time will depend on the size of your potato chunks). Drain the potatoes in a colander, leave them to steam dry for 10 minutes, then tip them back into the dry pan. Mash until smooth. Add the butter and cheddar, and lemon juice to taste, stir, then season with salt and white pepper. If the consistency is too stiff for piping, adjust with a little milk or cream. Set aside while you make the filling.

Melt the 2 tablespoons of butter in a saucepan over a medium heat. Add the flour and whisk to a paste, then leave the flour to cook out for a few minutes (it should darken and lose its floury smell). A little at a time, add the milk, whisking all the while, until you have added it all and the sauce is smooth. Leave the sauce to simmer and thicken for a few minutes, then remove it from the heat. Add the cheese, stirring to melt, and season with salt, pepper, and nutmeg if you wish.

Stir the white fish through the sauce. Reserve a few prawns for decoration, then stir the remainder of those through the sauce, too.

Heat the oven to 220°C/200°C fan.

To assemble the gratin, if you have a piping bag, fit it with a large closed star nozzle. Spoon in the mash and pipe it around the edge of a 2-litre, round baking dish in concentric circles to form a 'crown' (or, simply spoon in the mash and make a hollow in the centre). Pour the fish and prawn filling into the centre to fill, then place the dish into the oven for 20–25 minutes, until the filling is piping hot and the top is golden and bubbling. Top with the reserved prawns, pop the gratin back in the oven for 5 minutes to colour them, then finish with some finely chopped dill, if you like.

— HELSTEKT PLATTFISK MED ROSTADE ROTFRUKTER OCH VITLÖK —
Whole Roasted Flatfish with Oven-baked Potatoes, Carrots and Garlic

Simple and full of flavour, this is exactly the kind of food I like to cook at home. Roasting a whole fish in a cast-iron pan (first on the hob, then in the oven) gives the fish a beautiful, crisp skin – the kind you would expect if you were instead cooking over fire.

SERVES 2–3

2–3 tablespoons olive oil
2 garlic cloves, thinly sliced
1 whole flatfish (plaice, turbot or sole), cleaned and scaled
½ lemon, plus more to garnish
a few thyme sprigs, leaves picked, plus more to garnish
flaky salt

FOR THE VEGETABLES
6–9 small, colourful carrots
2–3 small potatoes, sliced
1 small onion, finely sliced
5 garlic cloves, peeled
olive oil, for drizzling
a few picked thyme sprigs

FOR THE DANISH REMOULADE
200ml mayonnaise
1 teaspoon mild curry powder
1 teaspoon Dijon mustard
2 tablespoons finely chopped gherkins or cornichons
1 tablespoon capers, rinsed and finely chopped
1 tablespoon finely chopped shallot or small onion
1 tablespoon chopped flat-leaf parsley leaves (or chives/dill)
1 teaspoon white wine vinegar
salt and white pepper

Heat your oven to 200°C/180°C fan.

Prepare the vegetables. Scrub the carrots clean. Place them with the potatoes, onion and garlic cloves into a baking dish, drizzle with olive oil, season with salt and sprinkle with thyme leaves. Bake for about 30–40 minutes, until softened and caramelised.

Meanwhile, make the remoulade. Combine the mayonnaise with the curry powder and mustard until smooth. Stir in the gherkins or cornichons, and the capers, shallot or onion, and herbs. Add the vinegar and season with salt and white pepper. Refrigerate the remoulade for 15–30 minutes while you cook the fish.

Heat an ovenproof, cast-iron frying pan or skillet over a high heat. Add 2 tablespoons of the olive oil, and, once hot, add the garlic. Fry until the garlic begins to smell (about 2–3 minutes), then add the fish (make sure you have enough oil in the pan – add a splash more if necessary, otherwise the fish will stick and the garlic burn). Fry for 2–3 minutes on each side, until nicely browned all over.

Remove the pan from the heat and squeeze over the juice from the lemon half. Add 2–3 tablespoons of water to the pan, season with flaky salt and sprinkle with the thyme leaves. Transfer the pan to the oven and cook for about 10–15 minutes, until the core temperature of the fish reaches 48–50°C at the thickest part – at which point the fish will be cooked but tender and juicy. The precise cooking time will depend on the size of the fish.

Serve the fish directly from the pan with the roasted carrots and potato. Top with spoonfuls of the remoulade and extra lemon and herbs, if you wish.

— **VARMRÖKT LAX MED POTATISSALLAD OCH INLAGDA RÖDBETOR** —

Hot-smoked Salmon Salad with Pickled Beetroots, New Potatoes and Parsley

Hot-smoked salmon is rich and warm with a delicate smoky flavour that is balanced by the brightness of the pickled beetroots. At the same time, the fish's flaky texture contrasts with the smooth texture of the new potatoes. This dish, with lots of balance and contrast, is wholly typical of how we eat in Sweden. It's the type of meal we'll often serve in summer, either at home, or as part of a buffet during the Midsummer festival.

SERVES 4

600g Charlotte potatoes
100ml crème fraîche
2 tablespoons chopped flat-leaf parsley leaves, plus more to serve
4 spring onions, finely sliced
2 tablespoons small capers, drained
300g hot-smoked salmon, flaked
4 pickled beetroots, sliced
salt and black pepper

Bring a large saucepan of salted water to the boil over a high heat. Add the potatoes and boil them for 20 minutes, or until soft. Drain the potatoes and leave them to cool, then cut them all in half.

Mix the potatoes with the crème fraîche, parsley, spring onions and capers and season with salt and pepper. Transfer everything to a serving plate.

Arrange the smoked salmon and beetroot slices on top of the potato salad and serve garnished with extra parsley sprigs.

TIP

Substitute smoked salmon with hot-smoked mackerel.

— GUBBRÖRA —

Swedish Anchovy and Potato Salad

The name *gubbröra* (literally, 'old man's mix') may come from the idea that this dish was eaten late at night, alongside a schnapps, by older gentlemen gathering to socialise. Certainly, the combination of anchovies, potatoes and eggs – all so readily available in Sweden – has existed in Swedish cuisine for a long time, first enjoyed as simple, salty food for fishermen and dockworkers. Despite its long history, *gubbröra* feels completely relevant, served at *smörgåsbords*, as a starter, or on a piece of crispbread at lunch.

SERVES 4

4 potatoes, peeled and chopped into 4cm cubes
2 eggs
200g Swedish anchovy fillets (below) or tinned sardines, drained and chopped
1½ tablespoons chopped dill
1½ tablespoons chopped flat-leaf parsley leaves
1 red onion, finely chopped
100ml crème fraîche
salt and black pepper
crispbread or rye bread, to serve

TO MAKE SWEDISH ANCHOVIES

30–40 drained anchovy fillets (or plant-based alternative)
4 teaspoons caster sugar
4 teaspoons distilled white vinegar (12% acidity)
3 small dried bay leaf, crushed
½ teaspoon allspice

Bring a small saucepan of salted water to the boil over a high heat. Add the potatoes and boil for 10–15 minutes, until they are just tender (the precise cooking time will depend on the size of your cubes – you want them cooked through but not soft). Drain the potatoes in a colander and leave them to cool. Further chop the cooled potatoes into 1cm cubes.

Meanwhile, bring a small pan of water to the boil. Carefully add the eggs, and boil for 10 minutes. Drain, leave to cool, then finely chop.

Layer the potatoes, eggs, anchovies, dill, parsley, onion and crème fraîche in a bowl (or into a pot for a portable lunch). Season with salt and pepper. Serve with crispbread or rye bread.

Swedish Anchovies (*Ansjovis*) in English Cooking

The term 'Swedish anchovies', as a translation, is confusing – what we want here is not the same as the anchovies typically available internationally. In Sweden, *ansjovis* (such as those of the brand Abba, which are available online) refers to a type of spiced and sweetened sprat, whereas the English 'anchovy' is a saltier and less-spiced fish. Swedish *ansjovis*, then, could be more accurately called 'Swedish spiced sprats' or 'Swedish anchovy-style sprats'.

If true Swedish anchovies are unavailable, substitute them with regular anchovy fillets, but you will need to adjust the flavour so that the result is both sweet and spiced. Add the ingredients noted (left) to your regular anchovies (leave them for a couple of hours in the mixture, if you can, before serving) to replicate our Swedish delicacy – the results won't be perfect but they will come close.

— JANSSONS FRESTELSE —

Potato and Swedish Anchovy Gratin

Potatoes, anchovies and onions baked in cream until everything melds together – you may know this dish as Jansson's Temptation. It is one of Sweden's most famous potato dishes, but its origins are debated. One theory is that it was named after the opera singer Per Adolf 'Pelle' Janzon, who was known for hosting lavish meals featuring anchovies and potatoes. Another explanation is that the name comes from the 1928 film *Janssons Frestelse*, during which the dish was supposedly served at a dinner party. Regardless of its origins, it is now staple fare at Swedish celebrations, especially at Christmas, Easter and Midsummer.

SERVES 4–6

800g potatoes (such as King Edwards or Russet), peeled
butter, for greasing, frying and dotting
2 onions, thinly sliced
200g Swedish anchovy fillets (see page 134), plus 1 tablespoon of the brine
150ml single cream
150ml whole milk
60g dried breadcrumbs
salt and black pepper

TIP

For a milder flavour, replace some of the anchovies with sardines in oil, or quickly rinse the anchovies before using, to reduce the saltiness.

Heat the oven to 200°C/180°C fan. Grease a 30cm x 20cm baking dish with butter.

Using a sharp knife, slice the potatoes into 3mm slices. Keep the slices together, then turn the potatoes and cut in the other direction at 3mm intervals, to give chips of potato. Once sliced, rinse the potatoes in cold water. Set aside.

Melt a knob of butter in a frying pan over a medium heat. Add the onions and fry for 5–7 minutes, until soft and translucent.

Layer the ingredients in the prepared dish like so: first, make a layer with half the potatoes, then a layer using all the onion, then add the remaining potatoes and finally the anchovies.

In a jug, combine the cream, milk and tablespoon of anchovy brine and pour the mixture over the contents of the dish. Sprinkle breadcrumbs evenly over the top and dot the topping all over with small pieces of butter.

Bake the dish for about 45 minutes, or until the potatoes are soft and the top is golden brown.

— FISKSOPPA MED SAFFRAN OCH FÄNKÅL —

Fish Soup with Saffron and Fennel

Inspired by Sweden's west coast, where seafood is king, this soup is both vibrant and fragrant. The fennel and saffron add depth, elegance – and a golden glow.

SERVES 4

1 tablespoon butter
1 leek, whites only, finely sliced
2 garlic cloves, minced
1 small fennel bulb, thinly sliced (keep any fronds for garnish)
1 carrot, diced (no need to peel)
1 teaspoon fennel seeds
½ teaspoon saffron threads
200ml dry white wine
1 tablespoon tomato purée
750ml fish stock
200ml double cream
400g skinless mixed fish fillets (such as cod, haddock and salmon), in 4–5cm chunks
200g peeled small prawns or cleaned, shell-on mussels
salt and black pepper
dill, fennel fronds or basil and lemon wedges, to serve

FOR THE HERB AÏOLI
2 egg yolks
1 teaspoon Dijon mustard
1 tablespoon white wine vinegar or lemon juice
200ml rapeseed oil
1 small garlic clove, grated
2 tablespoons very finely chopped dill
1 tablespoon very finely chopped parsley (optional)
white pepper

First, make the aïoli. In a bowl, whisk together the egg yolks, mustard and vinegar or lemon juice. Whisking constantly, drop by drop begin adding the oil. Then, when the mixture starts to thicken, you can increase the oil to a thin, steady stream. Once you have added all the oil and you have a thick and glossy mayonnaise, stir in the garlic and herbs and season to taste with salt and white pepper. Leave the aïoli to rest in the fridge for at least 30 minutes before serving, and while you make the soup.

In a large saucepan, melt the butter over a medium heat. Add the leek, garlic, fennel and carrot. Cook for 5–6 minutes, until softened.

Add the fennel seeds and saffron, then pour in the white wine. Simmer for 2–3 minutes, then stir in the tomato purée, stock and cream. Bring the mixture to a gentle boil, reduce the heat to a simmer and simmer for 10 minutes. Add the fish and cook for 5 minutes, then add the prawns or mussels. Put the lid on the pan and cook until all the fish is just done (about 5–10 minutes more).

Season to taste, then serve in bowls with spoonfuls of the aïoli and garnished with the dill, fennel fronds or basil, and with lemon wedges for squeezing.

— LAXPUDDING —

Salmon Pudding

A traditional Swedish comfort dish, *laxpudding* is simple, honest and deeply satisfying. You're going to boil the whole, peeled potatoes before slicing them, so try to choose some of similar size in order that they cook evenly.

SERVES 4

butter, for greasing and dotting
700g potatoes (such as Desirée), peeled but left whole
600g skinless salmon fillet, sliced across the grain into approximately 5mm slices
1 small onion, finely sliced
1 tablespoon finely chopped dill or flat-leaf parsley leaves
4 eggs
400ml whole milk or single cream (or a mixture)
salt and black pepper

Heat the oven to 220°C/200°C fan. Grease a 20–24cm diameter ovenproof dish (about 5cm deep) with butter.

Bring a large saucepan of salted water to the boil over a high heat. Add the potatoes and boil for about 15 minutes, until tender but not collapsing (the time it takes will depend on the size of your potatoes). Leave the potatoes to cool, then cut them into 5mm–1cm slices.

Cover the bottom of the dish with a layer of potatoes, slightly overlapping them as you go (aim to use about one third of the slices). Add a layer of salmon and onion, using half of each, season with salt and pepper and sprinkle with dill or parsley. Repeat, creating another layer each of potato, salmon, onion and seasoning and herbs, then finish with a final layer of potatoes.

Whisk together the eggs and milk or cream in a jug until combined. Pour the mixture over the layers. Dot the top of the pudding with butter and bake it for 35–40 minutes, or until the custard is set and golden.

Serve warm, preferably with clarified butter (see page 40) drizzled over and a spoonful of green peas or pickled cucumber.

Meat

In Scandinavian cuisine, there aren't actually that many luxurious dishes. Instead, Swedish food is *lagom*, a conflation of the words *lag* and *om* (see page 21). But that term itself is derived from *laget runt*, meaning everyone gets an equal share. It's not too much, not too little – it's just right. Nothing could be much more Swedish than that. Food should be humble and enough for everyone, which is something that comes up time and again in this chapter.

When it comes to Swedish meat dishes, meatballs are without a doubt the most iconic. It's the dish many people think of when they think of Sweden – just as legendary as ABBA and Volvo. I love meatballs! I've been eating them since I was a child, freshly fried straight from the pan when my grandmother was at the stove. It is something that many Swedes share as their first food memory. If we have a national dish, it's surely the meatball!

And if you want to find the most famous recipe for meatballs, look for Tore Wretman's version. He was Sweden's first celebrity chef, enjoying his heyday when my parents were young. The meatballs on page 169 are inspired by him, but with my own twist.

Meat

But this chapter is not only about what you might already know. I have also used it to re-introduce some Swedish meat dishes that I think have fallen out of favour – ones I had in school when I was little, or that my parents lovingly prepared at weekends. These dishes might not be as popular as they once were, but with an update – a modern twist – they represent delicious food worthy of its place.

My version of cabbage rolls (see page 155) is a bit simpler and quicker to make than a traditional version; and the Cabbage Pudding with Kale and Lingonberries on page 176, which used to take three hours, you can now rustle up in just one. I don't think that makes the dishes any less satisfying; quite the opposite. In modern times, cooking, and life, are different from when my grandmother stood by the stove and had all day to prepare the family meal. Today, we typically have just an hour (if that) to get a meal on the table. There's nothing wrong with that – rather, it has inspired me to simplify these classic dishes to better suit modern and busy lives.

So, this chapter is full of my takes on our classics: cabbage rolls, meatballs with lingonberries, Wallenbergare, fried pork with onion sauce, pork chops with apples, beef tenderloin with green pepper sauce, game stew, liver pâté, blood pudding and so many more – and they just happen to be some of my favourites, too.

— KYCKLINGLEVERPASTEJ —
Chicken Liver Pâté

Pork pâté on crispbread, often with pickles, was a staple of my childhood, but here I'm using chicken. This version shows up every Christmas at my house — and at other times of year when I fancy something rich and simple. It is smoother than the pork pâté of my youth, but has all the flavours it needs to conjure up plenty of happy memories. I'm serving it with berry compôte, but, of course, pickles would do just as nicely.

MAKES ABOUT 12 SLICES

400g chicken liver, chopped into small pieces
1 teaspoon salt, plus more to season
350g butter, at room temperature
1 shallot, finely chopped
50ml Cognac
½ teaspoon black pepper, plus more to season

TO SERVE
brioche, sliced and toasted
berry compôte or lingonberry jam, or pickles

Tip the liver into a bowl and season with the 1 teaspoon of salt. Set aside.

Heat 1 tablespoon of the butter in a frying pan over a medium heat. When melted and hot, add the liver and fry, turning occasionally, for about 3 minutes, until coloured all over and slightly pink in the middle. Lower the heat and add the shallot, frying for 2 minutes, until softened. Pour in the Cognac and add the pepper. Leave to simmer for 2 minutes, until the alcohol evaporates. Remove the pan from the heat and leave the mixture to cool slightly.

Tip the liver mixture into a food processor or blender and blitz it to a smooth paste. Little by little, with the motor running, add the remaining butter through the feed tube until you have a smooth and glossy pâté. Taste and adjust the seasoning if necessary.

Line a 750g terrine mould with a double layer of cling film, making sure to leave plenty overhanging the sides, and fill with the mixture. Smooth the surface and tighten the cling film over the top. Place the terrine in the fridge for at least 4 hours to chill and set, but ideally overnight.

Serve from the fridge, on toasted brioche with a tangy berry compôte or lingonberry jam, or pickles.

— STEKT FLÄSK MED LÖKSÅS, MAJS OCH SKIVAT ÄPPLE —
Fried Pork with Onion Sauce, Corn and Sliced Apple

To me, this is typical, everyday food – quick to prepare and wonderfully satisfying. With few ingredients, it is also probably one of the simplest dishes you'll come across in Swedish home cooking. You can substitute the pork with bacon if that's what you have on hand. And don't be put off by the thought of making an onion sauce – it is just onions, milk and a little flour; no fuss. Sweetcorn and sliced apple add a touch of sweetness and freshness, but at its core, this is a dish built on salt, fat and soft, comforting flavours – and it needs little else.

SERVES 4

500g salted pork, cut into 3mm-thick slices, or streaky bacon
1 tablespoon vegetable oil
2 onions, sliced
1 tablespoon plain flour
200ml whole milk
100ml double cream
300g frozen sweetcorn kernels
1 apple, peeled, cored and thinly sliced (reserve a couple of skin-on, whole slices for garnish)
a few picked mint leaves, to garnish

Heat a dry, non-stick frying pan over a medium–high heat. When hot, add the pork slices or bacon and fry for 5–7 minutes, until the fat has rendered, the meat is golden brown and cooked through and the edges have gone crispy. Remove from the pan and cover with foil to keep warm.

Heat the oil in a medium saucepan over a medium heat. Add the onion and fry for 6–8 minutes, until soft. Add the flour, then pour in the milk and cream and bring the mixture to a simmer, stirring continuously, until it thickens to the consistency of double cream (about 5 minutes). Add the corn kernels and apple slices and fold everything together. Leave the sauce for 5 minutes, until the corn is heated through, then serve topped with the pork and reserved thinly sliced apple and garnish with the picked mint.

TIP

Add a little Dijon mustard to the onion sauce for extra flavour.

— SNABBA KÅLDOLMAR —

Quick Cabbage Rolls

All the flavour of Swedish *kåldolmar* without the time-consuming, precision folding. This is an easy weeknight version of traditional, far more labour-intensive cabbage rolls. Tender cabbage still cradles spiced mince, but you fold loosely here, or serve them in an open, oven-roasted form. Either way, they are easy and delicious.

SERVES 4

butter or oil, for greasing
1 head of white cabbage
400g pork or beef mince, or a mixture
1 small onion, finely grated
1 egg, lightly beaten
100g cooked white rice
1 teaspoon ground allspice (optional)
2 tablespoons golden syrup
salt and black pepper
finely chopped chives, to garnish

Heat the oven to 200°C/180°C fan. Grease a baking tray or roasting tin with butter or oil.

Carefully remove 8–10 of the largest outer cabbage leaves (reserve the rest of the cabbage for another meal).

Bring a large saucepan of salted water to the boil over a high heat. Add the leaves and blanch them for 1–2 minutes, until soft and pliable. Drain and set aside.

In a bowl, mix the minced meat with onion, egg, rice and allspice (if using), and season with salt and pepper. Mix in the syrup.

One leaf at a time, hold the leaves in the palm of your hand and place a generous spoonful of the mixture into each centre. Fold in the ends and roll the leaf around the filling, just like you were folding and rolling a bread wrap. Place each filled leaf seal-side downwards in the baking tray or roasting tin and repeat until you've used all the leaves and filling. Don't worry if the rolling isn't perfect – a rustic look is fine. Alternatively, you can dispense with the rolling altogether: simply line the tray or tin with the cabbage leaves and use each one as a cup for the filling, open-style.

Transfer the tray or tin to the oven and bake the filled leaves for 25–30 minutes, until the meat is cooked through and the edges of the cabbage leaves are golden.

Sprinkle with chives to garnish and serve with boiled potatoes.

— STEKTA KOTLETTER MED SAUTERAD SPENAT OCH PÄRON —
Sautéed Spinach with Pears and Pork Chops

Pork chops are one of those ingredients that can easily turn dry without proper cooking. If you get them right, though, they become one of the easiest and tastiest dishes to prepare. I like to give the meat a proper sear, then let it rest well, ensuring it retains its juiciness. Here, the pork chop is served with sautéed spinach and pears, creating a perfect balance between saltiness and sweetness. The pears add a modern touch to this dish, but at its core, this is simple and delicious Swedish home-cooking.

SERVES 4

- 1 tablespoon olive oil, plus more for the spinach
- 1 small red onion, cut into 6 wedges
- 3 garlic cloves, peeled but whole
- 4 bone-in pork chops (about 3cm thick), at room temperature
- 2 pears, cored and cut into thin wedges
- 200g spinach
- salt and black pepper
- 4 tablespoons wholegrain mustard

Heat the oil in a frying pan over a medium–high heat. When hot, add the onion, garlic and pork chops. Fry everything together, turning the chops after 5 minutes. Add the pear slices and sauté for another 5 minutes, until the chops are fully cooked through and golden all over.

Season everything with salt and pepper and remove the meat, onions, garlic and fruit from the pan on to warmed serving plates. Leave to rest for 10 minutes.

In the same pan, add a little extra oil and sauté the spinach for about 3 minutes, until just wilted. Serve the spinach as a bed for the pork chops and pears. Top with spoonfuls of wholegrain mustard to serve.

TIP

Add a splash of balsamic vinegar to the spinach for extra acidity.

— LÅNGKOKT FLÄSKLÄGG MED ROTMOS —

Slow-cooked Pork Shank with Mashed Root Vegetables and Watercress

This is probably my father's signature dish and the one he always boasted about when I brought friends home. He knew it would be a hit and everyone would feel nostalgic as they tucked in. It's also perfect sustenance ahead of long hikes or working in the garden, as the meat and mash keep you going all day. If you can't find salted pork shank, you can brine the shank yourself in salted water for about two days (see below).

SERVES 4

1kg salted pork shank or ham hock
a few bay leaves (optional)
500g swede or celeriac, peeled and cut into 3–4cm cubes
300g potatoes, peeled and cut into 3–4cm cubes
200g carrots, peeled and cut into 3–4cm chunks
100g butter
a handful of watercress
a small handful of chives, finely chopped
salt and black pepper
wholegrain mustard, to serve (optional)

Place the pork in a deep pot. Pour in enough water to cover the meat, then place the pot over a medium heat. Add the bay leaves (if using), and a few grindings of black pepper, if you wish, then bring the water to the boil. Reduce the heat and simmer until the meat falls off the bone (about 2–3 hours).

Towards the end of the cooking time, bring a separate saucepan of salted water to the boil over a high heat. Add the chopped vegetables and boil for 8–10 minutes, until everything is soft. Drain and leave to steam dry in the colander for 10 minutes, then tip them back into the dry pan. Add the butter, and mash all the vegetables together with a potato masher – finish off with a balloon whisk for a super-smooth texture, if you wish. Season with salt to taste.

Spoon the mash into a serving bowl and top with the meat and watercress, then sprinkle with chives. Add spoonfuls of mustard, too, if you wish.

To make a brine

To make your own brine, measure out enough water to completely cover the shank. For every litre of water, add 100g of salt. Stir to dissolve the salt and add a bay leaf and peppercorns if you wish, then pour it into a container large enough to hold both the brine and the shank. Submerge the shank in the liquid, put the lid on the container and refrigerate for 2 days, turning after a day. Rinse off the brine before cooking as described in the recipe.

TIP

Add some grated horseradish to the mash for a spicy kick.

— KROPPKAKOR —
Swedish Dumplings with Meat Filling

The most beautiful island in the Baltic is Öland. Not only is it known for its stunning landscapes, but also most definitely for its *kroppkakor*.

SERVES 4 (MAKES ABOUT 24)

FOR THE DOUGH
800g starchy potatoes (such as Russets or King Edwards), peeled
1 egg
200–250g plain flour
salt

FOR THE FILLING
1 tablespoon butter, plus more to fry (optional) and to serve
1 small onion, finely chopped
200g cooked pork or bacon, finely chopped
½ teaspoon allspice (optional)
salt and black pepper

TO SERVE
butter, melted
lingonberry or redcurrant jelly
fried lardons (optional)

Begin with the dough. Bring a large pan of salted water to the boil over a high heat. Add the whole potatoes and boil for 20 minutes, or until soft. Drain well, leave them to steam dry for 10 minutes, then mash them thoroughly using a potato masher until smooth (or use a ricer). Tip the mash into a mixing bowl and leave it to cool.

Meanwhile, make the filling. Melt the butter in a large frying pan over a medium heat. Add the onion and fry for 5–7 minutes, until soft and translucent. Add the meat and allspice, cook for 5 minutes, until the pork is heated through or the bacon is cooked, then season to taste with salt and pepper. Leave the mixture to cool.

To finish the dough, crack the egg into the bowl with the mash, add 200g of the flour and season with salt. Mix to combine to a soft dough, adding the extra flour a little at a time and kneading until the dough is soft and no longer sticky (you may not need all the flour).

Divide the dough into about 24 equal portions. Form each portion into a ball, then flatten it a little and make a thumbprint hollow in the centre. Place 1 tablespoon of the filling into the hollow, then gather the sides over the filling to enclose, pinching the edges of the dough together in a tight seal. Repeat for all the portions of dough.

Bring a large saucepan of salted water to the boil over a high heat. Add the dumplings and boil for about 8–10 minutes, until they float to the surface – this tells you they're ready.

Scoop out the dumplings. If you like, at this point you can briefly fry them in a little butter over a medium heat, turning until golden. Either way, serve them dowsed in warm, melted butter with spoonfuls of lingonberry or redcurrant jelly on the side. A topping of crispy, fried lardons is tasty, too, if you like.

— GRILLADE FLÄSKKOTLETTER MED KRÄMIG SPETSKÅL —
Grilled Pork Chops with Creamy Pointed Cabbage

Stewed potatoes or vegetables have always been traditional in Swedish cuisine. We also eat stewed macaroni and mushrooms. When I was younger, our stews usually came in a rich béchamel sauce. Now, I love stewed vegetables, but I don't think they need to be swimming in a thick sauce. So, as I grew up and started working in restaurants, I replaced the heavy sauce with a few drops of cream instead. In this recipe, just a little cream at the end is enough to create a silky texture. A sprinkle of crushed pepper to finish completes the deliciousness.

SERVES 4

- a little vegetable oil, for brushing
- 4 bone-in pork chops (about 3cm thick), at room temperature
- 2 tablespoons unsalted butter
- 1 pointed cabbage, sliced into 2cm strips
- 100ml single cream
- 1 tablespoon Dijon mustard
- a small handful of tarragon, leaves picked
- salt and black pepper

Heat the grill to medium–high.

Brush the chops with a little vegetable oil and place them on the grill pan. Grill for 5 minutes each side, until fully cooked through. Remove the chops from the grill and season with salt and pepper. Keep warm.

Melt the butter in a large frying pan over a medium–high heat. Add the cabbage and sauté for 3–4 minutes, stirring occasionally, until wilted and just tender. Add the cream and mustard, and let the mixture simmer for a few minutes to heat through.

Divide the cabbage between your serving plates and top with a pork chop (slice it, if you wish). Garnish with a few tarragon leaves to finish.

TIP

Swap pointed cabbage for milder savoy cabbage as an alternative, if you wish.

— KÖTTBULLAR MED POTATIS, LINGON OCH INLAGD GURKA —

Swedish Meatballs with Potatoes, Lingonberries and Pressed Cucumber

Meatballs, or *köttbullar*, might just be the most Swedish thing there is. As soon as someone finds out you're Swedish, they ask: 'Can you make meatballs? What's your family recipe?' I've no doubt that IKEA can take most of the credit for the international stardom of Swedish meatballs – their most iconic product alongside flat-pack furniture. For me, though, meatballs are deeply connected to home and family. The recipe we serve in my restaurants comes from the renowned chef Tore Wretman, who was active in Stockholm during the 1960s and '70s. Wretman used his mother's recipe, which has since become a sort of gold standard for meatball-making among many Stockholm chefs. It's also the recipe I'm sharing here. What makes it stand out is Wretman's use of veal. In Swedish households, it's more common to use a combination of pork and beef.

Interestingly, the English equivalent of *köttbullar* isn't really meatballs as you probably think of them. A more fitting term would be 'meatbuns' – they are lighter and softer than you might expect. The base consists of cream, breadcrumbs and onion, and the mixture is beaten with a wooden spoon until smooth. Don't worry if your meatballs aren't perfectly round – a slightly uneven edge just adds to their charm. I highly recommend serving these with lingonberries (or cranberries, if you can't find lingonberries) – their sweet and tart flavour brings balance. In Sweden, it's common to serve meatballs with pickled cucumber – a touch of acidity to cut through the richness of the meat.

SERVES 4

about 2–3 tablespoons butter
1 onion, finely chopped
50g fresh breadcrumbs
100ml whole milk
500g mixed mince (veal, beef and pork is delicious)
1 egg, lightly beaten
800g potatoes, peeled and chopped into 4cm chunks
a small handful of flat-leaf parsley, leaves picked and finely chopped
1 cucumber, very thinly sliced

Melt 1 tablespoon of the butter in a frying pan over a medium heat. Once hot, add the onion and fry for 5–7 minutes, until soft and translucent. Leave to cool.

Tip the breadcrumbs into a medium mixing bowl and add the milk. Leave the breadcrumbs to swell for 5 minutes, then add the mince, egg and fried onion, and season with salt and pepper. Mix thoroughly with a wooden spoon until the ingredients are fully combined and the mixture is smooth.

Tear off a golf-ball-sized piece of the mixture and roll it between your palms to make a sphere. Repeat until you have used all the

...recipe and ingredients continued overleaf

2 tablespoons white wine vinegar
2 tablespoons caster sugar
2 tablespoons vegetable oil, plus more if needed
200g lingonberries (defrosted if frozen)
salt and black pepper
grated nutmeg, to serve

mixture – you should get about 12–16 meatballs altogether. Place them on a baking tray and refrigerate for 1 hour to firm up.

Meanwhile, heat a large saucepan of salted water over a high heat. Add the potatoes and boil for 15–18 minutes, until soft (the precise cooking time will depend on the size of your chunks). Drain the potatoes in a colander and leave them to steam dry for 10 minutes, then tip them back into the dry pan and mash them using a potato masher or ricer. Stir through the parsley. Set aside.

Put the cucumber slices in a bowl, then add the vinegar and sugar and 100ml of water, stir to combine and leave the slices in the liquid for at least 30 minutes to pickle.

Melt another tablespoon of butter with the vegetable oil in a frying pan over a high heat. When hot, add the chilled meatballs and fry, turning regularly, for 2–3 minutes, or until browned all over and cooked through – you can cut a meatball in half to check, there should be no pink or red and the juices should run clear. You may need to do this in batches (adding more oil and butter, as necessary), depending on the size of your frying pan. Make sure there is enough room for the meatballs to turn easily, otherwise they will steam rather than fry. Keep each cooked batch warm while you fry the remainder.

Serve the meatballs with the pickled cucumber and mash, and scatter with the lingonberries. Finish with a good grating of nutmeg over the meatballs and cracked black pepper over the mash.

TIP

Use lingonberry jam instead of lingonberries if you want to balance out the meatiness with a little extra sweetness. If you can't find lingonberry jam in your region, cranberry sauce makes a good substitute.

— BLODPUDDING —
Blood Pudding

For me, blood pudding is a trip back to my mother's kitchen. I doubt I am alone: most people in Sweden grow up with blood pudding as a family staple, or as children, enjoyed it on the regular rotation of school meals. Its sweet flavour is certainly appealing to a child's sweet tooth! Commonly, blood pudding is eaten with lingonberries and cottage cheese, and that's exactly how I love it – and with bacon, too. Getting hold of pig's blood can be a bit tricky, but talk to your butcher – it's absolutely worth the effort.

MAKES ABOUT 12 SLICES

500ml pig's blood (or use lamb's or sheep's), strained
350ml mild beer (or any stock)
210g coarse rye flour
1 red onion, finely chopped
50g unsalted butter, melted
50ml golden syrup
½ teaspoon ground ginger
¼ teaspoon white pepper
¼ teaspoon ground allspice or 5-spice
a pinch of ground cloves
1 teaspoon salt
50g lardo cubes or unsmoked bacon lardons
boiling water
vegetable oil

TO SERVE (OPTIONAL)
crispy fried bacon bits
lingonberry jam
4 tablespoons cottage cheese
a small handful of mustard cress

TIP

Apple sauce makes a delicious alternative to lingonberry jam.

Heat the oven to 180°C/160°C fan. Grease a 1.5-litre terrine mould or loaf tin with butter (or use two 750g moulds or tins if you prefer).

In a bowl, mix the blood with the mild beer (or stock) and rye flour. Add the onion, butter, golden syrup, ginger, white pepper, allspice or 5-spice, cloves and salt. Whisk the mixture vigorously, then stir in the lardo or lardons to evenly distribute.

Pour the mixture into the prepared tin. Then, grease a sheet of baking paper and lay it greased side down on top of the mixture inside the tin. Cover with foil.

Set the loaf tin inside a deep roasting tray and fill the roasting tray with boiling water so that it comes halfway up the sides of your loaf tin. This acts as a water bath to cook the pudding evenly.

Transfer the pudding in the water bath to the oven and bake it for 1 hour, until cooked through – check with a skewer or knife by piercing the centre. If the skewer or knife comes out clean (no wet residue), the pudding is done. (If you're using two smaller terrine moulds, test each one after 50 minutes.) Remove the pudding from the water bath, but leave it covered to cool in the tin. Once cool, refrigerate it (still covered) overnight to chill and set.

To serve, turn out the pudding from the tin and cut it into 2cm-thick slices. Heat a little vegetable oil in a frying pan and fry the slices for 2–3 minutes on each side, until charred and hot through. Serve with crispy fried bacon pieces and lingonberry jam; or with lingonberry jam mixed with cottage cheese and spooned over crispbread. Scatter with mustard cress to finish.

— KÅLPUDDING MED GRÖNKÅL OCH LINGON —

Cabbage Pudding with Kale and Lingonberries

Where the British have Cottage Pie, the Swedes have Cabbage Pudding. Layers of cabbage, rice and mince, this simple weeknight supper makes the most of staple ingredients, with fruit for a bit of zing. Use any type of plain, unflavoured rice – I usually use some left over from another meal. For the minced meat, mixed mince (usually beef and pork) works well, but you can use one or the other, if you prefer. Sometimes I use lamb, which is very tasty.

SERVES 4

100g rice (use your favourite, but jasmine works well), or use 250g leftover cooked rice
500g minced meat of choice
1 head of cabbage (any is fine), chopped into small chunks
salt and black pepper

TO SERVE
200g lingonberries (defrosted if frozen)
200g kale, tender leaves picked and torn

Unless you're using leftover cooked rice, cook the rice according to the packet instructions until tender, then drain it.

Tip the cooked rice into a bowl with the minced meat and mix them together to fully combine. Set aside.

Heat the oven to 200°C/180°C fan. Grease a 30cm x 20cm baking dish with butter.

Bring a large saucepan of salted water to the boil. Add the cabbage and blanch for 3 minutes, until tender.

Layer the cabbage and meat mixture in the baking dish, beginning with the meat/rice and finishing with a layer of cabbage. Bake the pudding for 45 minutes, until cooked through and golden.

Meanwhile, massage the torn kale leaves with a little salt to soften, then set aside.

Serve the pudding with lingonberries scattered over and the softened kale leaves on the side.

TIP

Drizzle about 4 tablespoons of golden syrup over the cabbage pudding before baking to give it an irresistibly sweet top.

— OXFILÉ MED ROSTADE ROTFRUKTER OCH TÄNDSTICKSPOTATIS —

Fillet of Beef with Roasted Root Vegetables and Crispy Potato Matchsticks

When I cook meat at home, I like to keep things simple. In this case, simple means a perfectly seared beef fillet served with deeply flavoured roasted root vegetables that have been tossed in a herby oil, and a crisp element for contrast – a topping of golden matchstick potatoes. It is just as fitting for a Friday night as it is for a festive gathering.

SERVES 4

sunflower oil, for frying
600g beef fillet, sliced into 4 equal portions, at room temperature
salt and black pepper

FOR THE ROASTED ROOT VEGETABLES
600g firm potatoes, peeled and cut into 2cm chunks
300g celeriac, peeled and cut into 2cm chunks
2 onions, peeled and cut into 2cm chunks
sunflower oil, for drizzling

FOR THE HERB OIL
about 50g flat-leaf parsley (add a few lovage leaves, if available, too)
200ml sunflower oil
1 tablespoon lemon juice

FOR THE CRISPY POTATO MATCHSTICKS
2 large, firm potatoes, peeled
sunflower oil, for deep-frying

First, prepare all the root vegetables. Heat the oven to 200°C/180°C fan. Spread the potatoes, celeriac and onions over a baking tray lined with baking paper. Drizzle with a little sunflower oil and season with salt and pepper. Roast in the middle of the oven for 30 minutes, or until golden on the outside and tender in the middle.

Meanwhile, make the herb oil. In a food processor, blitz the parsley (and lovage, if using) with the oil until smooth and green. Add the lemon juice and season with salt. Set aside until needed.

Using a mandoline or sharp knife, cut the potatoes into 2mm slices. Keep the potato stacks together, then use a sharp knife to slice in the opposite direction at 2mm intervals to give fine matchsticks. Rinse in cold water and dry thoroughly on kitchen paper.

Half-fill a deep saucepan with sunflower oil and heat it to 140°C on a cooking thermometer (or use a deep-fat fryer). Add the matchsticks and fry for 5 minutes, until soft, but not yet golden. Scoop them out on to kitchen paper to drain. While they are draining, increase the heat of the oil to 180°C. Tip the matchsticks back into the oil and fry again for 2–3 minutes, until golden and crispy. Set aside to drain and season with salt. Keep warm while you cook the beef fillets.

Heat a large frying pan with a little sunflower oil over a high heat. Add the fillets and sear quickly on each side until browned. Season with salt, reduce the heat, and cook, turning occasionally, until the internal temperature of each fillet reaches 52°C (for medium–rare). It should take about 2–3 minutes on each side. Remove the beef to a plate, season with pepper and leave to rest for 10 minutes.

Toss the roasted vegetables in the herb oil to coat. Divide them equally between your 4 serving plates, place the beef fillet on top, then pile with the crispy matchsticks. Serve immediately.

— TOAST PELLE JANZON —

Toast Pelle Janzon

This 19th-century Swedish classic is named after opera singer Pelle Janzon. It is luxurious, elegant and distinctly Nordic. The traditional way to serve it is to entirely hide the bread using the meat – a surprise to be uncovered!

SERVES 4

200g high-quality beef fillet or sirloin
butter, for frying
4 slices of white sourdough bread or brioche
1 small red onion, finely chopped
1 tablespoon finely chopped chives
4 tablespoons vendace roe or trout roe
4 small egg yolks (preferably organic)
flaky salt and freshly ground black pepper
a few drops of mild olive oil or lemon juice, to serve (optional)

First, prepare the meat. Using a very sharp knife, very thinly slice the beef, carpaccio-style, so that it is almost translucent. Place the slices between sheets of baking paper as you go. When you have finished, gently pound the slices using a rolling pin to get them thinner if needed. Transfer the slices to the fridge to chill while you make the remaining elements of the dish. (You can ask your butcher to slice your beef, if you prefer.)

Melt the butter in a frying pan over a medium heat. When hot, add the bread slices and fry for 2–3 minutes on each side until golden and crispy. Do this in batches, if necessary, adding more butter as you go. Leave the slices to drain on kitchen paper.

To assemble, divide the bread slices between 4 serving plates. Top each with equal amounts of the beef, arranging the slices to make them look beautiful and entirely covering the bread.

Combine the onion and chives in a bowl and divide them between the beef slices. Add a dollop of roe in the centre, then an egg yolk. Season with salt and pepper. A few drops of olive oil or lemon juice can help to bring out the flavours. Serve immediately as a starter, ideally with a cold lager or a glass of wine.

— BIFF RYDBERG MED PERSILJA OCH STEKT ÄGG —

Biff Rydberg with Parsley and Fried Egg

Biff Rydberg is essentially a deconstructed *pyttipanna*, which is a kind of hash. It uses the same ingredients – meat, potatoes, onions and eggs – just not mixed together. The potatoes are fried separately, the onions cooked on their own, and the meat has its own place on the plate. I like this dish because of its simplicity. No sauces, no embellishments – just good ingredients. Be mindful to fry the onions slowly until they are deeply caramelised and sweet, which balances the saltiness of the meat and potatoes. Here, I've used beef, but you can easily replace it with game. Top the lot with a fried or raw egg and a heavy sprinkling of parsley, and it's ready to serve.

SERVES 4

1 tablespoon butter, plus more for frying the onions and eggs
2 tablespoons vegetable oil
600g beef fillet or sirloin steak, diced into 2cm cubes
800g King Edward or Russet potatoes, peeled and cut into 2cm cubes
2 onions, chopped
4 eggs
salt and black pepper
a small handful of flat-leaf parsley, tender sprigs picked, to serve

TIP

A dollop of Dijon mustard on each serving can bring out the savouriness of the meat and add a tangy quality to the whole dish.

Melt the butter with the oil in a frying pan over a medium heat. When hot, add the beef cubes and fry, turning, for 3–4 minutes, until browned on all sides (how long the meat will take to cook to your liking will depend on its quality – the better the quality, the quicker the cooking time). Scoop the fried meat out of the pan and set it aside on a plate to keep warm.

Tip the diced potatoes into a colander and rinse them under cold water, then pat them dry with kitchen paper. Tip them into the hot pan and fry for 4–5 minutes, until tender, golden and crispy (it's important that your pieces of potato are uniform to ensure even cooking and a crispy surface). Scoop them out and set them aside.

Add a little more butter. When it has melted and is hot, add the onions to the pan and fry over a medium heat for 5–7 minutes, until soft and translucent. Set aside with the potato cubes.

Finally, add a little more butter to the pan, break in the eggs and fry them for 7–8 minutes over a medium heat, until the whites are set but the yolks are still runny.

Divide the beef equally between 4 serving plates or bowls. Add a portion of potatoes and onions alongside and top the potatoes with a fried egg. Add the parsley to serve.

WALLENBERGARE MED GRÖNA ÄRTER, PEPPARROT OCH CITRON
Fried Wallenbergare with Peas, Horseradish and Lemon

There are some dishes that hold a special place in my heart – Wallenbergare (named after a member of Sweden's famous Wallenberg family) is one of them. Another symbol of Swedish comfort food, these are luxurious, velvety patties made with minced veal, cream, egg yolks and a touch of seasoning – they should almost melt in your mouth. For me, though, this is more than just a meal; it is tradition and elegance. For the best results, make sure all your ingredients are very cold when you mix them, which stops the meat and cream separating. Keep the mixing bowl cold, too – refrigerate it for 30 minutes first. For the best texture, I prefer to use a food processor than to mix by hand. Typically, Wallenbergare comes with mashed potatoes, lingonberries and green peas. In this version, I'm sticking with peas and dispensing with potatoes and lingonberries. If I do serve it with potatoes, I prefer it with boiled new, rather than mash.

SERVES 4

500g veal mince
2 egg yolks
200ml single cream
200g panko breadcrumbs
1 tablespoon butter
2 tablespoons vegetable oil
200g peas
salt

TO SERVE

1 tablespoon grated horseradish
1 lemon, sliced into wedges
a sprinkling of chopped flat-leaf parsley leaves (optional)

TIP

Swap veal mince for chicken mince for a lighter version. And, if you prefer, you can make your meatballs bigger – just adjust the cooking time accordingly.

Tip the mince into a food processor and add the egg yolks. Start the motor on low speed, then gradually add the cream through the feed tube. Once all the cream has been incorporated, season with salt and form the mixture into 10–12 equal patties – each the size of a small hamburger. Set aside on a plate.

Tip the breadcrumbs into a shallow bowl. One by one, coat the patties on both sides, setting them aside as you go.

Melt the butter with the oil in a large, deep frying pan over a medium–high heat. Once hot, add the patties (in batches, if necessary), frying for 5–7 minutes on each side until golden brown all over and cooked through.

Meanwhile, bring a pan of salted water to the boil over a high heat and add the peas. Boil for 3–4 minutes, until tender, then drain.

Serve the Wallenbergare with the grated horseradish sprinkled over and lemon wedges for squeezing over. Add the peas on the side, mixed through with parsley, if you wish.

— HJORTFILÉ MED HASSELBACKSPOTATIS OCH STEKT SVAMP —

Hasselback Potatoes with Fried Venison Fillet and Mushroom Compôte, Sage and Thyme

All the things I love on one plate: mushrooms, crisp potatoes and game meat. Hasselbacks are named for the Hasselbacken Hotel in Stockholm, where they were popularised in the 1950s. They make for an elegant side, but I like them as a snack, too.

SERVES 4

FOR THE HASSELBACKS
800g waxy potatoes (such as Charlotte)
50g butter, melted
10g dried breadcrumbs
1 teaspoon salt
30g mature cheddar cheese, grated (optional)

FOR THE VENISON FILLET
600–700g venison fillet
15g butter
a few sage and thyme sprigs
salt and black pepper

FOR THE MUSHROOM COMPÔTE
10g butter
1 small shallot, finely chopped
250g mixed mushrooms (such as chanterelles, white button or trompettes), finely diced
150ml double cream
a few picked thyme sprigs

FOR THE SALAD
1 head of Romaine lettuce, torn
40g croûtons
2 teaspoons olive oil
100g small cauliflower florets (optional, shaved)
a few dill fronds

To make the hasselbacks, heat your oven to 240°C/220°C fan. Place each potato between two chopsticks or wooden-spoon handles to avoid cutting through completely and slice them thinly (at about 2mm intervals) along their length. Brush with melted butter.

Place the potatoes in a roasting dish and sprinkle with the breadcrumbs, salt, and cheese (if using). Bake for 30–40 minutes, until crispy on top and tender on the insides. Meanwhile, make the other elements of the dish.

Season the venison fillet with salt and pepper.

Melt the butter in a frying pan over a medium heat and, when hot, fry the fillet on all sides until a nice brown crust forms. Add the sage and thyme to the pan, then fry for a further 10–12 minutes, or until the core temperature of the meat reaches 58–60°C (this will give you medium–rare). Set aside the meat somewhere warm to rest, then clean the pan ready to make the compôte.

To make the mushroom compôte, melt the butter in the clean frying pan over a medium heat. When hot, add the shallot and fry for 2 minutes, until soft. Add the mushrooms and fry for 3–4 minutes, until they release their juices and are slightly browned. Add the cream, season with salt and pepper and sprinkle in the thyme. Let the sauce simmer for another 5 minutes, then remove from the heat but keep warm.

To make the salad, toss all the ingredients together in a bowl, season with a pinch of salt, and set aside.

To serve, divide the mushroom compôte between 4 serving plates. Slice the venison fillet and arrange the slices over the mushrooms. Add the potatoes, and serve with the salad. Enjoy!

— **VILTGRYTA MED BRYSSELKÅL OCH KÅLRABBISALLAD** —

Creamy Game Stew with Brussels Sprouts, Sunflower Seeds and Kohlrabi Salad

In Sweden we have a dish called *renskav* or *viltskav*, which is often the first dish containing wild meat that children try. It's a creamy game stew simply served with mashed potatoes or rice, and it's frequently eaten at school, or at home during weekdays. Even though I've always enjoyed this stew, and despite the fact it's probably the most common way Swedes eat game meat, I find it a bit plain. So, I serve it with a really good salad, which makes it much tastier.

SERVES 4

vegetable oil, for frying
600g game meat (such as elk, venison, lamb or duck), cut into 2–3cm chunks
1 onion, sliced
100g crème fraîche
200ml single cream
200g Brussels sprouts, trimmed
5–10 chanterelles mushrooms, chopped
2 tablespoons sunflower seeds
1 kohlrabi, peeled and thinly sliced
1 tablespoon white wine vinegar
salt and black pepper
finely chopped dill, to serve

TIP

If you prefer, swap the toasted sunflower seeds for toasted pumpkin seeds.

Heat a little oil in a large frying pan (choose one with a lid) over a high heat. Once hot, add the game pieces and the onion and fry, turning regularly, until the meat is seared on all sides and the onion is browned – about 4 minutes.

Add 100ml of water to the pan, along with the crème fraîche and cream, and mix everything together. Reduce the heat, put the lid on the pan and let it all simmer for 1 hour, stirring occasionally to stop it catching, until the meat is tender and cooked through.

About 10 minutes before the end of the stew cooking time, bring a saucepan of salted water to the boil over a high heat. Add the sprouts, and boil for about 8 minutes (the exact cooking time will depend on the size of your sprouts), until soft. Drain them, then tip them into a small frying pan with a little oil and fry briefly over a medium–high heat until just coloured. Tip them into a serving bowl. Toss the mushrooms into the pan to colour a little, then add them to the bowl with the sprouts – they will soften in the residual heat.

Just before the stew is ready, heat a dry frying pan over a medium–high heat. Add the sunflower seeds and toast them for 2 minutes, until golden and aromatic. Immediately tip them on to a side plate to stop them cooking (they will burn quickly) and set them aside.

In a serving bowl, toss the kohlrabi in the white wine vinegar and season with salt and pepper, to make a salad.

Taste, season, then spoon the stew into bowls and sprinkle with the seeds and dill. Serve with the salad and the bowl of sprouts and mushrooms on the side.

FIKA

I once had a conversation with a well-known baker from Sweden – someone I have admired for a long time and followed closely, both on social media and through his cookbooks. His bread recipes are among the best I know, and they have inspired me in many ways. During our conversation, he said something that made me pause for a moment: 'A Swedish bakery wouldn't be able to survive without cinnamon buns.'

That comment put things into perspective for me. Cinnamon buns are more than just pastries in Sweden – they are a cultural icon. Swedes are obsessed with them; they are an intrinsic part of everyday life. We eat them often, not just on special occasions but as part of our routine. And it's not just us Swedes who appreciate them: tourists flock to bakeries to taste our iconic buns, then document the experience with photos. It's not even unusual to see long queues outside some popular bakeries, where people eagerly wait to get their hands on a coveted, celebrated cinnamon bun.

For me, then, cinnamon buns are a clear symbol of Sweden and I love them as much as anyone else. But, if I'm honest with you, I have another favourite: the cardamom bun. As a Stockholm native, I'm not alone in this – it's almost an unwritten rule here that those who choose a cardamom bun over a cinnamon bun are locals. I find it amusing to sit in a café and watch how customers choose their buns. It often reveals a lot about them. (You can find my recipes for each on pages 197 and 257, respectively.)

Happily, baking at home has once again become very popular in Sweden, largely thanks to social media, with quick recipe videos showing just how easy it is to prepare and bake snacks and treats. I love to see how many people are rediscovering the joy and creativity that's to be found in transforming humble ingredients into something delicious.

In Sweden, baking is never more needed than it is for our ritual of *fika*, a concept deeply rooted in our culture. So much more than the opportunity for something sweet with coffee, *fika* is a way to take a break, to relax and to socialise. In our daily lives, *fika* is almost as important as breakfast – it's one of the strongest social rituals Swedes have. Whether it happens on a Sunday afternoon or as a quick pause during the workday, *fika* is an integral part of life across the whole country.

In addition to *fika*, we have *mellanmål* (snack), something eaten between breakfast and lunch, or between lunch and dinner. When I was little, *mellanmål* was that crucial titbit that would keep up our energy levels until supper. I always had *mellanmål* at school, and then again at home, where my mother was careful that whatever she gave us wasn't too sugary. Today, many people choose ready-made, store-bought options for *mellanmål*, but I believe those snacks rightfully deserve to come from the kitchen.

Whether you bake to have something to offer at your next *fika* or to enjoy a homemade stop-gap before supper, you can be sure there is magic in what you will make. And, to return (almost) to where we started: if there is one treat that remains the most magical of all treats for me, it's the cardamom bun. This chapter is full of many of my favourite pastries and snacks, but I urge you, of course, to turn to that page first.

— **KANELBULLAR MED HASSELNÖTSFYLLNING** —

Cinnamon Buns with Hazelnuts

The cinnamon bun is a now beloved staple everywhere, but a hundred years ago it was very much considered a luxury. After World War I, when sugar and butter became more readily affordable again, Swedes started baking sweet yeast doughs flavoured with cinnamon — a spice that itself had long been both expensive and exotic. Now, in Sweden, the cinnamon bun is more than just a pastry; it is part of our culture. We even celebrate Cinnamon Bun Day every year, on 4th October.

MAKES 15

25g fresh yeast or 7g instant dried yeast
250ml whole milk
75g unsalted butter, softened
50g caster sugar
1 teaspoon ground cardamom
325g plain flour (or use bread flour), plus more for rolling
pearl sugar, for sprinkling (optional)

FOR THE FILLING
75g unsalted butter, softened
2 tablespoons ground cinnamon
50g caster sugar
25g hazelnuts, finely chopped

Crumble the fresh yeast into a mixing bowl or tip in the dried (use the bowl of a stand mixer if you have one).

Pour the milk into a small saucepan and place it over a medium–low heat. Warm the milk gently until it reaches 37°C on a cooking thermometer ('blood' temperature — just lukewarm to the skin). Pour the milk into the bowl with the yeast and stir to dissolve. Add the butter, sugar, cardamom and flour and combine to a homogenous dough.

By hand, or in a stand mixer fitted with the dough hook on medium speed, knead the mixture for 5 minutes, until smooth and elastic. Cover the bowl with a clean tea towel, set it aside, and leave the dough to rise for about 45 minutes in a warm place, until doubled in volume.

Line two baking trays with baking paper, and, in a bowl, combine the butter and cinnamon for the filling until evenly mixed.

Remove the risen dough from the bowl and gently form it into a rectangle. With a floured rolling pin on a lightly floured work surface, roll out the dough to a rectangle measuring 35cm x 25cm. With a long side closest to you, spread the spiced butter over the dough in an even layer, leaving a 1cm border around the edge. Sprinkle evenly with the caster sugar and hazelnuts

...continued overleaf

Pick up the closest long edge of the dough and roll it on to the filling, as tightly as you can all along the length. Roll all the way to the opposite edge to create a log. Turn the log so that the seam is underneath. With a sharp knife, trim each end to neaten. Discard the trimmings, then cut along the length of the roll to create 15 equal slices.

Turn the slices so that the spiral is facing upwards and place each on a lined baking sheet, spacing the pieces about 5cm apart so that they join together as they prove. Cover the tray with a tea towel and leave them to prove at room temperature for 30 minutes, until puffed and each one is nudging the next.

Meanwhile, heat the oven to 250°C/230°C fan.

Once the rolls are puffy, transfer the baking sheets to the oven and bake the rolls for 10–12 minutes, until golden, squishy and cooked through. Sprinkle with pearl sugar, to decorate, if you wish.

The buns will keep in an airtight container for up to 3 days. Refresh them in a warm oven before serving, if you like. Alternatively, you can freeze the unbaked slices for up to 6 weeks and bake from frozen – just give them a little longer in the oven.

TIP

Brush the buns with sugar syrup after baking and before you sprinkle them with pearl sugar to give them a gorgeous shine (it will also give the sugar pearls a better stick).

— VANILJBULLAR —
Vanilla Buns

To me, vanilla buns are the slightly more luxurious cousin of the cinnamon bun – soft, fluffy and loaded with a sweet vanilla filling. But the best part of a vanilla bun is the playful challenge that comes with eating it. When I was a child, we would dare each other to eat a whole bun without licking our lips. Sounds easy, but when your lips are covered in sugar crystals, trust me – it is almost impossible. Like all the best games, the challenge inevitably ended in laughter – and conceding defeat halfway through so that we could just enjoy the eating.

MAKES ABOUT 15

25g fresh yeast or 7g instant dried yeast
250ml whole milk
500g plain flour (or use bread flour)
75g caster sugar
1 teaspoon ground cardamom
75g unsalted butter, at room temperature
1 teaspoon salt

FOR THE CREAM FILLING
125ml whole milk
a pinch of vanilla powder or ½ vanilla pod
2 tablespoons caster sugar
2 egg yolks
2 teaspoons cornflour
25g unsalted butter, softened

TO FINISH
25g unsalted butter, melted
50g caster sugar

First, make the filling. Heat the milk with the vanilla in a saucepan over a medium heat until the milk just starts to boil. Immediately remove the pan from the heat.

In a bowl, whisk together the sugar, egg yolks and cornflour. Stir continuously as you pour in the warm milk (remove the vanilla pod, if necessary).

Return the pan to a medium–low heat and stir until the mixture thickens to the consistency of custard (don't let it get too thick, as it will firm up further when the buns bake). Add the butter, then stir to melt and combine.

Pour the cream filling into a cold bowl. Cover the surface with cling film to stop a skin forming, then refrigerate until needed (alternatively, you can dispense with the cling film and just stir frequently as it cools).

To make the buns, crumble the fresh yeast into a mixing bowl or tip in the dried (use the bowl of a stand mixer if you have one).

Pour the milk into a small saucepan and place it over a medium–low heat. Warm the milk gently until it reaches 37°C on a cooking thermometer ('blood' temperature – just lukewarm to the skin). Pour the milk into the bowl with the yeast and stir to dissolve. Add the flour, sugar, cardamom, butter and salt and mix to a homogenous dough.

...continued overleaf

By hand or in the bowl of a stand mixer fitted with the dough hook on medium speed, knead for about 10 minutes until smooth and elastic. Cover the bowl with a clean tea towel, and leave the dough to rise in a warm place for about 30 minutes, until doubled in volume.

Meanwhile, line two baking trays with baking paper.

Divide the risen dough into 15 equal pieces and roll each piece into a ball. Place the balls on the lined baking trays, spacing them well apart. Once you have rolled them all, cover the trays with a clean tea towel and leave the balls to prove in a warm place for 40 minutes until risen.

Heat the oven to 200°C/180°C fan. Spoon the vanilla cream filling into a piping bag fitted with a plain 3cm nozzle (if you don't have one, you can spoon the cream into the buns, so don't worry).

Press your thumb gently into the middle of each bun to create a hollow and pipe or spoon in the vanilla cream.

Bake the buns in the middle of the oven for 7–9 minutes, until golden. Remove the trays from the oven and leave the buns to cool. Once cooled, brush them with the melted butter and roll them in the 50g of caster sugar to finish. The buns will keep in an airtight container for up to 4 days.

201

203

— BLÅBÄRSMUFFINS —

Blueberry Muffins

Blueberries are one of Sweden's most treasured ingredients – wild, free and bursting with flavour. For generations, we have picked them in the forests, then eaten them straight from our hands, or taken them home to use in jams, pies and other bakes. Muffins, however, are far from Swedish. They originated in America but quickly became a favourite here, perhaps because they are so easy to make and lend themselves perfectly to blueberries. In this recipe, the best of both worlds meet – the Swedish wild berries and the moist American muffin. It is a bake that feels both new and familiar, tasting exactly as a great *fika* moment should.

MAKES 12

240g plain flour
170g granulated sugar, plus more for the topping
a pinch of salt
2 teaspoons baking powder
100g butter or margarine, melted
100ml whole milk
2 eggs
200g frozen blueberries (do not thaw)

Heat the oven to 220°C/200°C fan.

In a mixing bowl, mix together the flour, sugar, salt and baking powder. Add the melted butter or margarine and stir to combine.

In a separate bowl, whisk together the milk and eggs, then add the mixture to the dry ingredients. Stir until just combined. Gently fold in the frozen blueberries, reserving a few for garnish.

Line a 12-cup muffin tray with paper muffin liners and divide the mixture equally between them. Toss the reserved blueberries in a little extra sugar and place a few on top of each muffin.

Bake the muffins in the middle of the oven for about 20 minutes, or until golden, and a toothpick inserted into the centre of each muffin comes out clean. The muffins will keep in an airtight container for up to 5 days.

TIP

Using frozen blueberries helps keep the fruit suspended in the muffin mixture as the muffins bake – so you won't end up with a layer of blueberries that have sunk to the bottom.

— TARTE TATIN MED PLOMMON —
Plum Tarte Tatin

Of course, we all know tarte tatin as a French dessert, but I chose to include it because it's incredibly delicious, beautiful to serve and timeless in its appeal. Inspiration often comes from beyond our own borders, and tarte tatin is one of those dishes I am more than happy to adopt into my world. It feels just as natural to serve after a Swedish Sunday dinner as any traditional Swedish cake. The recipe is for one large tatin, but you could make four smaller ones if you prefer – each to share between two.

SERVES 8–10

16 plums (any kind is fine), halved and pitted
1 x 320g sheet of puff pastry (defrosted if frozen)
200g caster sugar
150g unsalted butter, cubed
vanilla ice cream, to serve

Place the plum halves cut side down in concentric circles in a 26–30cm-diameter ovenproof frying pan. Gently lay the sheet of puff pastry over the top to test the fit – if necessary, roll it a little wider and trim the corners so that the sheet is just larger than the circumference of the pan. Set the pastry aside again for now.

Tip the sugar into a small saucepan and place it over a medium heat. Leave the sugar to melt and colour without stirring, until it turns golden brown (about 5–7 minutes). Watch the pan carefully and don't let the sugar burn. Add the butter – be cautious because the caramel will bubble and spit – then stir until smooth.

Remove the pan from the heat and immediately pour the caramel evenly over the plums in the frying pan. Cover the plums with the sheet of pastry, tucking the edges neatly inside the rim of the pan.

Place the pan into the oven and bake the tatin for 20 minutes, until the pastry is golden and cooked through.

Protecting your hands, remove the pan from the oven. Place a serving plate (larger than the size of the pan) top down on top of the pan and, holding the plate in place, quickly invert it all to remove the tart to the serving plate, plums upwards. Leave to cool briefly, then serve in wedges with vanilla ice cream.

— TEKAKOR MED SMÖR OCH DROTTNINGSYLT —

Swedish Flatbreads with Queen's Jam and Butter

Soft, slightly sweet flatbreads, *tekakor* have been a staple in Swedish baking for generations. Despite their name, which translates as 'tea cakes', they are not pastries but rather a type of bread, traditionally enjoyed for breakfast or *fika*. The name *tekaka* (the singular form) likely comes from the influence of British tea culture, which gained popularity in Sweden during the late 19th and early 20th centuries. As Swedish home-baking evolved, these soft, round breads became a beloved alternative to the more common crisp or dense rye loaves, and were perfect for spreading with butter and jam. In this recipe, I pair *tekakor* with Queen's Jam – a classic Swedish blend of blueberries and raspberries – along with butter. It's a taste of Sweden's baking heritage, where tradition meets everyday comfort.

MAKES 15–20

50g fresh or 14g instant dried yeast
500ml whole milk
150g unsalted butter, softened
750g plain flour, plus more for rolling
1 teaspoon salt
Queen's jam and butter, to serve

Crumble the fresh yeast into a mixing bowl or tip in the dried (use the bowl of a stand mixer if you have one).

Pour the milk into a small saucepan and place it over a medium–low heat. Warm the milk gently until it reaches 37°C on a cooking thermometer ('blood' temperature – just lukewarm to the skin). Pour the milk into the bowl with the yeast and stir to dissolve. Add the butter, flour and salt and mix to combine to a dough.

By hand, or in a stand mixer fitted with the dough hook on medium speed, knead the dough for 5 minutes, until smooth and elastic. Cover the bowl with a clean tea towel and leave the dough to rise in a warm place for about 30 minutes, until almost doubled in volume. Meanwhile, heat the oven to 250°C/230°C fan. Line two baking trays with baking paper.

Turn out the risen dough on to a lightly floured work surface and roll it out until it's about 2cm thick. Using a large teacup, cut out 15–20 rounds from the dough, re-rolling the trimmings, and spacing the flatbreads well apart on the trays. Cover the baking trays loosely with a clean tea towel and leave the rounds to prove in a warm place for 30 minutes, until almost doubled again.

Prick the risen flatbreads all over with a fork. Place the baking trays in the oven and bake the flatbreads for 10–15 minutes, until light golden brown. Leave the flatbreads to cool a little, then slice them in half and serve warm with Queen's jam and butter.

— CHOKLADBOLLAR —
Chocolate Balls

Requiring no eggs or flour, *chokladbollar* date from the early 20th century, when oats became a common ingredient in Swedish home-baking because wartime rationing made more usual baking ingredients hard to find or expensive. Now they are among Sweden's most beloved no-bake treats (no wonder – they are irresistible), a staple addition to Swedish *fika*, and are to be found in nearly every café, bakery and home. They are made from just a few pantry staples – oats, butter, sugar, cocoa and coffee – rolled into bite-sized balls and coated in desiccated coconut or pearl sugar. They couldn't be simpler.

MAKES ABOUT 25

200g unsalted butter, softened
200g caster sugar
250g porridge oats
6 tablespoons cocoa powder
2 teaspoons vanilla sugar
4 tablespoons brewed coffee, cooled
pearl sugar or desiccated coconut, for rolling

Mix the butter, sugar, oats, cocoa powder, vanilla sugar and coffee together in a mixing bowl until everything is fully combined.

Tip the pearl sugar or coconut on to a shallow saucer.

Wet your hands a little to stop the mixture sticking. Pick up a piece of the mixture and roll it between your palms into a ball – you want enough that the result is just smaller than a golf ball. Place the ball in the pearl sugar or coconut in the saucer and roll it around to fully coat. Transfer the ball to a plate lined with baking paper and set it aside while you roll the remainder. You should get about 25 balls altogether.

Place the plate in the fridge and chill the balls for at least 1 hour before serving. They will keep in an airtight container in the fridge for 3–4 days (or as long as the use-by date on your butter).

TIP

Replace the coffee with orange juice for a delicious chocolate orange version.

— TUNNBRÖD —

Flatbread

This bread is a true piece of my homeland! Growing up in Jämtland, in the northwest, I developed a deep love for *tunnbröd* – an essential part of northern Swedish cuisine. Wonderfully versatile, where I come from *tunnbröd* is not served only alongside soups and stews, it's also used as a vessel for a sort of hot-dog wrap. A *tunnbrödsrulle*, filled with sausage, mashed potatoes, and perhaps a spoonful of prawn salad, is a favourite after a long day – or a night out. To me, this bread is one of the most genuinely Swedish things there is.

MAKES 15–20

50g fresh or 14g instant dried yeast
600ml whole milk
100g butter, softened, plus optional extra to serve
750g rye flour
150g plain flour, plus more for rolling
2 teaspoons salt
sea salt, to sprinkle (optional)

TIP

To cook the flatbreads in an open wood oven, place the grid over the glowing embers and put the rolled-out flatbreads on top. Cook for 2 minutes on each side, until charred all over and puffed.

Crumble the fresh yeast into a mixing bowl or tip in the dried (use the bowl of a stand mixer if you have one).

Pour the milk into a small saucepan and place it over a medium–low heat. Warm the milk gently until it reaches 37°C on a cooking thermometer ('blood' temperature – just lukewarm to the skin). Pour the milk into the bowl with the yeast and stir to dissolve. Add the butter, rye flour, plain flour and salt and mix to combine to a dough.

By hand, or in a stand mixer fitted with the dough hook on medium speed, knead the dough for 5 minutes, until smooth and elastic. Cover the bowl with a clean tea towel and leave the dough to rise slightly at room temperature for 30 minutes.

Divide the dough into 15–20 equal pieces and roll each piece into a ball. Cover the balls with the tea towel. Then, one by one, using a rolling pin, roll out the balls on a lightly floured work surface, each to a circle about 25–30cm in diameter (you want each disc to fit comfortably in your frying pan). Set each rolled flatbread aside covering them with a clean cloth, as you go.

Heat a dry frying pan over a high heat. One at a time, fry the flatbreads for 1–2 minutes on each side, until puffed and lightly charred all over. Serve immediately, or wrap them in a tea towel and keep them warm in a low oven until you're ready. Serve the flatbreads as they come, or brush them with butter and sprinkle with sea salt, if you like.

— SAFFRANSBULLAR —

Saffron Buns

Golden, scented with saffron, and shaped into beautiful S-shaped spirals, these buns are a Swedish Christmas essential. Made for St Lucy's Day on 13th December, as they bake they fill the house with warmth and light during our darkest time of year. For me, saffron buns taste like childhood mornings, candlelight and the quiet joy of waiting for snow.

MAKES 20

25g fresh yeast or 7g instant dried yeast
200ml whole milk
0.5g saffron
¼ teaspoon salt
100g caster sugar, plus more for finishing
120g quark (10% fat) or 25g room-temperature unsalted butter
75g unsalted butter, at room temperature
500g plain flour (or use bread flour), plus more for rolling

FOR THE FILLING
200ml whole milk
5 tablespoons instant custard powder

TO FINISH
1 egg, beaten
15g unsalted butter, melted

Start with the filling. Mix the milk and custard powder in a bowl until it thickens, then cover and refrigerate to set (about 2 hours).

About 1 hour into the chilling time, make the dough. Crumble the fresh yeast into a mixing bowl or tip in the dried (use the bowl of a stand mixer if you have one). Pour the milk into a small saucepan, add the saffron and place the pan over a medium–low heat. Warm the milk to 37°C on a cooking thermometer ('blood' temperature – just lukewarm to the skin). Pour the milk and saffron into the bowl with the yeast, and stir to dissolve. Add the salt, sugar and quark or 25g of butter to the bowl, then mix to combine. Add the 75g of room-temperature butter. A little at a time, add the flour, mixing well between each addition, then knead by hand or with the dough hook on medium speed for about 10 minutes, until smooth and elastic. Cover the bowl with a tea towel, and leave the dough to rise in a warm place for about 45 minutes, or until doubled in volume.

On a lightly floured work surface, roll out the dough to a 30cm × 40cm rectangle. Spread the filling evenly over the top, to the edges. With a short edge closest to you, fold the bottom third up, then fold the top third down, like folding a letter. Roll again, this time to a 20cm × 40cm rectangle, to flatten and secure the layers.

If necessary, turn the dough so a long edge is closest to you. Using a sharp knife or pizza cutter, cut 20 strips, each about 2cm wide. Twist each strip along its length, then coil each end in opposite directions to make an 'S' shape. (At other times of year, simply coil the twisted strips into a spiral for a non-Christmas version!)

...continued overleaf

Line two baking trays with baking paper and place the buns on top, spacing them out evenly (they will expand as they prove). Cover each tray with a tea towel and leave the buns to prove for 30 minutes. Heat the oven to 220°C/200°C fan. Brush the proved buns with beaten egg, then bake for 10–12 minutes, or until golden and cooked through. Leave to cool slightly, then brush with melted butter and sprinkle with sugar before serving. Once cooled, they will keep in an airtight container for up to 3 days (refresh them in a warm oven).

TIP

Turn leftover buns into crispy rusks. Slice them and bake the slices at 150°C/130°C fan until crisp. A perfect topping for blueberry soup (see page 86)!

— VÄSTERBOTTENSPAJ —

Swedish Cheese Pie

I come back time and again to this pie (or, in the more English sense, tart). It is as much a staple at a crayfish party as it is at a simple dinner with friends. Creamy, salty and full of flavour, it is also ridiculously easy to make. Traditionally, we make it with Västerbottensost, a Swedish hard cheese with a sharp, salty character. You might find Västerbottensost difficult to track down outside Sweden, so a well-aged cheddar or gruyère works just as well. I like to serve the tart warm, with a dollop of crème fraîche and a sprinkling of red onion. If you want to make it more festive, add some bleak roe.

SERVES 8–10

FOR THE PASTRY
350g plain flour, plus more for rolling
250g butter, cubed and chilled

FOR THE FILLING
6 eggs
400ml single cream
400g Västerbotten (or use well-aged cheddar or gruyère cheese), grated
salt and white pepper

FOR THE TOPPINGS (OPTIONAL)
a bunch of radishes, trimmed and halved (keep the leaves)
a few handfuls spinach
dollops of crème fraîche, to serve
a few spoonfuls of bleak roe

First, make the pastry. In a bowl, rub together the flour and butter until the mixture resembles breadcrumbs. Add 2 tablespoons of water and bring the mixture together into a ball of dough. Wrap the dough in cling film and rest it in the fridge for 30 minutes. Meanwhile, heat the oven to 220°C/200°C fan. Grease a 28cm loose-bottomed tart tin (5cm deep) and line it with baking paper.

Once the dough has rested, roll it out on a lightly floured work surface to a circle large enough to fit the tin neatly with a little overhang. Carefully transfer the rolled-out dough to the tin, draping it over the rim and leaving gravity to let the middle sag into the hollow. Gently ease the pastry into the corners. Trim any excess.

Place a piece of scrunched-up baking paper into the centre of the tart case and fill with baking beans or rice. Blind bake the pastry case for 10 minutes, until lightly golden. Remove the beans or rice and paper and trim the pastry edge to neaten (or leave it rustic, if you prefer). Leave the case to cool slightly and leave the oven on.

While the pastry case is cooling, make the filling. In a bowl, whisk together the eggs and cream and stir in the cheese. Season with salt and pepper. Pour the filling into the cooled pie crust (it won't fill all the way to the top, which leaves room for extra toppings), and bake for 30 minutes, until the filling is puffed and golden with a slight wobble in the centre, and the pastry edge is deep golden.

Leave the tart to cool in the tin, then remove it and transfer it to a serving plate. Top the tart with your choice of extras – radishes and their reserved green tops and spinach are a good option, with crème fraîche alongside. Or try bleak roe on a special occasion.

— **FYRA SORTERS SMÖRREBRÖD OCH ETT HEMBAKAT RÅGBRÖD** —

Open Sandwiches on Rye Bread

There are few things as deeply rooted in both Danish and southern Swedish lunch culture as *smörrebröd* – the open sandwiches. They are simple food, but at the same time, an art form. On a dark, dense rye bread, layers of flavour, texture and colour – often with fish, liver pâté, boiled eggs and seasonal vegetables (asparagus in spring, beetroots in autumn) – make the most beautiful and inviting light snack. Each one should look a bit luxurious, but beneath there is a humble base. What's great about *smörrebröd* is that there are almost no rules – just a sense of balance and tradition. And one more thing: they are always eaten with a knife and fork. Preferably with a cold beer and a small shot of something.

Here, I've made four open sandwiches – one with radishes and cottage cheese, one with beetroots and mushrooms, one with chicken liver pâté and pickles, and one with boiled eggs and pickled fried herring. All are served on a coarse Danish rye bread. Of course, you can buy the bread, if you like, but just in case you want to make your own, a recipe for rye bread is over the page and is based on a classic version from Arla.se, adjusted to my measurements.

ALL MAKE ONE OPEN SANDWICH

1 slice of Danish rye bread
40g cottage cheese
2–3 radishes, thinly sliced, with leaves
salt and black pepper

Radishes and Cottage Cheese

Place the rye bread on a serving plate and spread the cottage cheese over the top. Add the radish slices and leaves. Season with salt and pepper. Simple flavours – but together, they are hard to beat.

1 slice of Danish rye bread
2 button mushrooms, sliced and sautéed in butter, then cooled
50g cooked beetroots, thinly sliced
salt and black pepper
a few edible nasturtiums, to decorate

Beetroots and Mushrooms

Place the rye bread on a serving plate and top with the mushrooms and beetroot slices. Season with salt and pepper and scatter with the edible flowers for a touch of elegance, to garnish.

...continued overleaf

1 slice of Danish rye bread
1 boiled egg, sliced
1 fillet of pickled fried herring
  (see page 109; warm or cold)
1 tablespoon mayonnaise
  (optional)
a few fresh chives,
  finely chopped

Boiled Egg and Pickled Fried Herring

Place the rye bread on a serving plate and top with the slices of egg. Top with the pickled herring and a little mayonnaise, if desired. Finish with a sprinkling of chives.

1 slice of Danish rye bread
1 teaspoon butter
40g chicken liver pâté
  (see page 150)
1 pickled baby cucumber,
  halved lengthways
2 pickled baby onions, halved
½ small roasted red pepper
  from a jar, chopped
1 teaspoon lingonberry jam
a little mustard cress or flat-leaf
  parsley, to garnish

Chicken Liver Pâté and Pickles

Place the rye bread on a serving plate and spread it with the butter. Add the pâté, then the pickles and pieces of red pepper. Season with salt and pepper, then finish with the lingonberry jam and cress or parsley, to garnish.

**MAKES 1 LOAF
(ABOUT 16 SLICES)**

400g coarse rye flour
100g plain flour
75g sunflower seeds
75g flax seeds (optional)
50g pumpkin seeds
2 teaspoons salt
1 teaspoon bicarbonate of soda
1 tablespoon black treacle
500ml buttermilk or yoghurt

Homemade Rye Bread

Heat the oven to 200°C/180°C fan. Grease a 1.5-litre loaf tin with butter.

Mix all the dry ingredients in a bowl and make a well in the centre. Add the treacle, buttermilk or yoghurt and 100ml of water and stir to incorporate until you have a thick batter.

Pour the batter into the prepared loaf tin and bake on the lowest shelf for about 1½ hours, until the top is darkened and the loaf is cooked through. Remove the tin from the oven and leave the loaf to cool in the tin completely before turning it out and slicing it. The bread will keep wrapped in a clean tea towel at room temperature for several days. Or, you can freeze it in slices with great results.

— KOLAKAKOR —

Caramel Cookies

Crisp and chewy, these cookies require only a few ingredients and are quick to bake, making them an almost instant *fika* favourite. They are perfect with coffee over the morning news, as a little everyday treat in a lunchbox, or when you want to offer something homemade for guests to enjoy with a glass of wine, without spending hours in the kitchen.

MAKES ABOUT 30

200g unsalted butter
200g caster sugar
250g plain flour, plus more for rolling
2 teaspoons vanilla sugar
2 teaspoons baking powder
2 tablespoons golden syrup

Heat the oven to 200°C/180°C fan and line two baking sheets with baking paper.

Mix the butter, caster sugar, flour, vanilla sugar, baking powder and syrup in the bowl of a stand mixer fitted with the dough hook on medium speed, or by hand in a bowl with a wooden spoon, for 5–7 minutes, until you have a smooth dough.

Turn out the dough on to a lightly floured work surface and divide it in half. Using your hands, roll each piece of dough into a log, about 30cm long and 3cm in diameter. Place the logs on to the prepared baking sheets spaced well apart and press them flat so that they are about 2cm thick.

Bake the flattened logs for about 10 minutes, until golden and crispy at the edges (the centres will still be a little soft, but they will harden while they cool). Remove from the oven and, while the logs are still warm, slice each one diagonally into 15 pieces, to give 30 biscuits altogether. Leave to cool completely. The cookies will keep in an airtight container for about 1 week; or you can freeze them for about 1 month.

TIP

A sprinkling of sea salt on the cookies before baking will give them a salted caramel flavour.

— HALLONGROTTOR —

Raspberry Dreams

Hallongrottor translates to 'raspberry caves' because raspberry jam nestles in a little biscuit well for these treats. In the USA and UK, you might know them as 'thumbprint cookies'. For me, as I think for many Swedes, *hallongrottor* are a childhood favourite. They are buttery and crumbly with a good chew. The tempting dollop of jam in the centre brings extra sweetness. Raspberry is the typical flavour for the jam, but you can, of course, experiment with others.

MAKES ABOUT 30

200g unsalted butter
350g plain flour, plus more for rolling/shaping
200g caster sugar
2 teaspoons vanilla sugar
2 teaspoons baker's ammonia
raspberry jam, for the filling

Heat the oven to 170°C/150°C fan and line two baking sheets with baking paper.

Mix the butter, flour, caster sugar, vanilla sugar and baker's ammonia in the bowl of a stand mixer fitted with the dough hook on medium speed, or by hand in a bowl with a wooden spoon, for about 5–7 minutes, until you have a smooth dough.

Turn out the dough on to a lightly floured work surface and divide it into about 30 pieces, each about the size of a walnut. Using your hands, roll each piece into a ball. Place the balls on to the prepared baking sheets, spacing them well apart. Using the back of a teaspoon, press down in the middle of each ball to flatten it slightly and to create a hollow. Fill each hollow with a teaspoonful of raspberry jam.

Bake the cookies for 15 minutes, until light golden at the edges and cooked through. Remove from the oven and leave to cool on the baking sheets before serving. The cookies will keep in an airtight container for 3–5 days; or freeze for up to 3 months.

TIP

Swap raspberry jam for Queen's jam – just as Swedish, but a twist.

— MJUKA MANDELKAKOR —

Soft Almond Cookies

In Sweden we have a tradition of taking a gift of a little something sweet when visiting friends. *Mandelkakor*, with their soft almond flavour and hint of bitter almond, are perfect for that. They're humble, nostalgic and often found on the table during a proper *fika*.

MAKES ABOUT 30

200g whole skin-on almonds
200g caster sugar
pared zest of 1 unwaxed orange
½ teaspoon ground cinnamon
2–3 egg whites
a few tablespoons of flaked almonds (optional)
icing sugar, to decorate

Heat the oven to 200°C/180°C fan. Line two baking trays with baking paper.

Process the almonds and sugar in a food processor until they are finely ground.

Add the orange zest, cinnamon and 2 of the egg whites. Process to a dough – if it's too crumbly, add another egg white (or a little water) and process again until the dough comes together. It should be firm enough to drop on to a baking tray without crumbling apart.

Drop equal spoonfuls of the dough on to the lined baking trays – you should get about 30 dollops in total. Sprinkle the mounds of dough with the flaked almonds, if using, then bake the cookies for 15 minutes, until golden and crisp on the outside but soft in the middle. Leave to cool, then dust with icing sugar to decorate and serve. The cookies will keep in an airtight container for 2–3 weeks, or for up to 6 months in the freezer.

— MOROTSKAKA MED CITRONFROSTING —
Carrot Cake with Lemon Frosting

In the 1980s, many food trends arrived in Sweden from the USA, and my mother was quick to pick up the trend for this moist cake, which would make an appearance as a real highlight at birthdays. She always made it with a generous amount of frosting – just as it should be. I've mostly kept her tradition, but sometimes I like to add a bit of ginger to the batter for more spice; or to make it a little more Swedish, I sometimes sneak in a smattering of cardamom (as here). It gives the cake a deeper flavour with a hint of familiarity. The frosting, of course, is the best part. I like to have plenty of it, with extra lemon for a fresh contrast. This cake tastes like family and home to me, but at the same time, it has become part of our Swedish *fika*. An American classic – with a Swedish twist.

SERVES 6–8

150g sunflower oil
175g unsalted butter, room temperature
400g caster sugar
4 eggs
300g carrots, peeled and grated
350g plain flour
1 teaspoon baking powder
1 teaspoon bicarbonate of soda
½ teaspoon salt
1 tablespoon ground cinnamon
2 teaspoons ground cardamom

FOR THE LEMON FROSTING
300g full-fat cream cheese
250g icing sugar, sifted
2 tablespoons vanilla sugar
pared zest of 2 lemons, plus optional extra to decorate
150g unsalted butter, melted

Heat the oven to 170°C/150°C fan. Line a 23cm springform cake tin (base and sides) with baking paper.

In a stand mixer fitted with the beater on medium speed, or by hand in a mixing bowl, whisk together the oil, butter and sugar until creamy – about 3–4 minutes. One at a time, add the eggs, whisking well between each addition. Using a spatula, fold in the grated carrots until evenly distributed.

In a separate mixing bowl, mix together all the remaining cake ingredients. Then, sift them into the bowl with the wet mixture and gently fold together to create a smooth batter with no dry patches remaining. Try not to over-mix, though.

Pour the batter into the prepared tin and bake it for about 1 hour, or until a cocktail stick inserted into the centre of the sponge comes out clean. Leave the sponge to cool for a few minutes in the tin, then release it and leave it to cool completely on a wire rack.

For the frosting, whisk together the cream cheese, icing sugar, vanilla sugar and lemon zest until smooth. Gradually add the melted butter, whisking all the time, until the frosting is fluffy and thick.

Top the cooled cake with the frosting and decorate with extra lemon zest, if desired. Serve in wedges and enjoy!

— CHOKLADSNITTAR —
Chocolate Slices

Thin crisp-edged slices of chocolate cookie, often topped with a sprinkle of pearl sugar, *chokladsnittar* are a classic on any Swedish cookie tray. We often bake them in long strips and slice them warm. Just like *mandelkakor* (see page 232), they're the kind of thing you bring along when visiting someone for coffee.

MAKES ABOUT 54

100g unsalted butter, at room temperature
100g caster sugar
1 egg yolk
150g plain flour, plus more for rolling
3 tablespoons cocoa powder
1 tablespoon vanilla sugar
½ teaspoon baking powder
egg white, for brushing
pearl sugar, for sprinkling

Heat the oven to 200°C/180°C fan. Line a large baking tray with baking paper.

In a stand mixer fitted with the beater on medium speed, or by hand in a mixing bowl, cream together the butter and sugar until smooth and creamy (about 3–4 minutes). Add the egg yolk and mix well. Add the flour, cocoa powder, vanilla sugar and baking powder and mix together to form a smooth dough.

Turn out the dough on to a lightly floured work surface and divide it into thirds. Roll each third into a log, about 2cm in diameter and about 40cm long. Place the logs on the lined baking tray about 5cm apart. Gently flatten each log so that it is 1cm thick, brush with egg white and sprinkle with pearl sugar.

Bake the logs for about 10–12 minutes, until they smell caramelised (take care not to overbake them – they are dark so you have to go by aroma), then remove the tray from the oven. While the logs are still warm, cut each one into 18 equal-sized diagonal pieces. Leave the pieces to cool on the tray. The slices will keep in an airtight container for up to 1 week, and for up to 2 months in the freezer.

— UGNSPANNKAKA —
Thick Pancake

This is the pancake I grew up with. Not the thin, crispy kind, but a thick, oven-baked version that is wonderfully fluffy in the middle and slightly crispy at the edges. It smells of childhood and weekday dinners – simple, satisfying and always delicious. It is baked in a single, large dish, making it perfect for days when you don't feel like frying pancakes one by one. I like to serve it traditionally with lingonberry jam or crushed, fresh berries, but sometimes I add grated cheese or fried bacon to the batter for a heartier, savoury version.

SERVES 4

3 eggs
100g plain flour
1 tablespoon caster sugar
½ teaspoon vanilla sugar
2 pinches of salt
200ml whole milk
40g unsalted butter

TO SERVE
berries of choice (crushed a little) or lingonberry (or your favourite) jam
plain yoghurt
maple syrup

Heat a 26cm cast-iron pan in the oven at 200°C/180°C fan.

Crack the eggs into a mixing bowl and whisk with a hand-held electric mixer until pale and frothy.

In a separate bowl, mix together the flour, caster sugar, vanilla sugar and salt. Alternating them one at a time, gradually add the flour mixture and the milk into the eggs, whisking until smooth between each addition until you have added everything and have a thick, smooth pancake batter.

Protecting your hands, take the hot pan out of the oven. Add the butter to the pan, and let it melt.

Pour the batter into the pan and bake it for about 20 minutes, until golden and puffed up.

Scoop the berries or jam into the centre and serve the pancake in wedges drizzled with yoghurt and maple syrup, too, if you like.

— FINSKA PINNAR —

Finnish Almond Biscuits

Finska pinnar have always been there. When I was little, they often appeared on the biscuit tray at family *fika* gatherings – perhaps not the first biscuit you'd reach for as a child, but one you learned to appreciate over time. You only truly realise how good they are when you take a bite. Crisp, buttery and with just the right amount of almond, they are simple with a touch of elegance. Despite their name, they are not particularly Finnish (*finska*), but Sweden and Finland have long shared culinary traditions, so it's not surprising that the biscuits ended up being attributed to our Scandinavian neighbour. To me, though, they are typically Swedish, and I like to make them with a little extra almond and a pinch of salt to enhance the flavours. They are perfect, as is so much *fika*, with a cup of coffee.

MAKES ABOUT 50-60

1 bitter almond, finely grated; or 2 drops of almond extract
200g butter, room temperature
300g plain flour, plus more for rolling
pinch of salt (optional)
40g caster sugar
1 egg, beaten, for brushing
a few tablespoons of flaked almonds (or use finely chopped blanched whole almonds, if you prefer), for sprinkling
pearl sugar, for sprinkling

Combine the bitter almond or almond extract in a food processor with the butter, flour, salt (if using) and sugar to form a dough. Bring the dough together into a ball with your hands, then wrap it in cling film and chill it for 30 minutes to 1 hour to firm up.

Meanwhile, heat the oven to 200°C/180°C fan. Line two baking trays with baking paper.

Turn out the dough on to a lightly floured work surface and divide it into 4 equal pieces. Roll each into finger-thick logs, about 60cm long.

Brush the logs with the beaten egg, then sprinkle with flaked (or chopped) almonds and pearl sugar. Cut each log into 4–5cm pieces. Place the pieces on the lined baking trays and bake in the centre of the oven for 9–10 minutes, until golden. Leave to cool before serving. They will keep in an airtight container for up to 3–4 days.

— FRÖKNÄCKE —

Seed Crispbread

I always have a batch of this in my kitchen. It's one of those things that feels deeply Swedish – simple, crunchy, full of seeds and care. I often break it into rough pieces and serve it with strong cheese and a cold beer, either before dinner or just when I need something savoury. Fröknäcke is part of the new Swedish pantry – rooted in tradition, but open to the world. And once you start baking it, you won't stop.

MAKES ABOUT 12

100g sunflower seeds
50g pumpkin seeds
50g flax seeds
50g sesame seeds
2 tablespoons chia seeds
200ml just-boiled water
1½ tablespoons rapeseed oil
1 teaspoon flaky sea salt

Preheat the oven to 200°C/180°C fan.

In a mixing bowl, mix together all the ingredients except the sea salt. Stir well and leave the mixture sit for 10–15 minutes so that the seeds swell and thicken.

Line baking tray with a sheet of baking paper. Scoop the mixture on to the paper and use a palette knife to spread it into an even layer over the entire surface of the paper. Place another sheet of baking paper on top and press the mixture out thinly using your hands.

Remove the top sheet of paper, sprinkle the cracker mixture evenly with the flaky sea salt and bake it in the middle of the oven for 40–45 minutes, until dry and golden. Remove the tray from the oven and leave the cracker to cool completely. It will harden as it cools. Once completely cold, break it into pieces. The crackers will keep in an airtight container in a dry place for up to 2 weeks.

— KLADDKAKA —
Swedish Chocolate Cake

If Sweden has an answer to a gooey chocolate cake, *kladdkaka* is it. This dense, rich cake is crispy on the outside and sticky in the middle, and the go-to dessert both for birthdays and for last-minute *fika*. Which is good, because it's also very easy to make.

SERVES 8–10

3 eggs
250g caster sugar
150g butter, melted
200g plain flour
50g cocoa powder
1 tablespoon vanilla sugar
lingonberries (defrosted if frozen), to decorate (optional)
icing sugar, for dusting
lightly whipped cream, or ice cream, to serve

Heat the oven to 220°C/200°C fan. Line the base of a 22cm springform cake tin with baking paper.

In a mixing bowl, lightly whisk together the eggs and caster sugar, then stir in the melted butter.

Sift the flour, cocoa powder and vanilla sugar into the mixture, and gently fold it all together into a smooth batter.

Pour the batter into the prepared tin and bake it in the lower part of the oven for about 12 minutes, until the cake is baked with a slight wobble in the centre (this will give you your gooey middle in the finished cake).

Let the cake cool completely in the tin, then release it and transfer it to a serving plate. Scatter over a handful of berries, if you wish, and dust over some icing sugar. Serve the cake in slices with lightly whipped cream, or ice cream.

— SEMLOR —
Swedish Semlor

Traditionally eaten on Fat Tuesday (our version of Pancake Day, at the start of Lent), *semlor* (singular: *semla*) are, in theory, a beloved seasonal Swedish treat – but, in reality, we start enjoying them weeks before Lent arrives. Pillowy and scented with cardamom, the buns are filled with almond paste and whipped cream, making them deeply indulgent. In Swedish homes, bringing *semlor* to a *fika* is a gesture of care and friendship.

MAKES 12

200ml whole milk
25g fresh yeast or 7g instant dried yeast
420g plain flour, plus more for kneading and shaping
1 egg, plus another (beaten) for brushing
½ teaspoon salt
1 tablespoon crushed cardamom seeds (not pre-ground)
85g caster sugar
100g unsalted butter, softened

FOR THE FILLING
50ml whole milk
75g almond paste (use good-quality shop bought, or homemade)
30g chopped almonds
200ml double cream, whipped to firm peaks
icing sugar, for dusting

Begin the dough. Warm the milk in a saucepan over a low heat to no more than 37°C ('blood' temperature – lukewarm to the skin).

If you're using fresh yeast, crumble it into the bowl of a stand mixer, or tip in the dried yeast, and stir in the warm milk until dissolved. Measure out 240g of the flour and add this to the bowl. Stir to combine and leave to rest for 15 minutes – this wakes up the yeast.

After the 15 minutes, add the remaining 180g of flour, along with the egg, salt, cardamom and sugar. Mix with a wooden spoon until combined. Place the bowl on the stand mixer and fit the dough hook. On medium speed, a little at a time, knead in the butter until it's all incorporated and you have a smooth, elastic dough. This should take about 7–10 minutes. (Alternatively, you can mix and knead by hand for a similar amount of time.) Cover the bowl with cling film or a tea towel and leave the dough to rise for 30 minutes.

Turn out the risen dough on to a lightly floured work surface and divide it into 12 equal pieces. Shape each piece into a ball and place the balls on a baking tray lined with baking paper, spacing them well apart (you will likely need two trays). Cover each tray with a tea towel and leave the balls to prove for 1½–2 hours, until doubled in volume. Towards the end of the proving time, heat the oven to 210°C/190°C fan. Brush the risen buns with the beaten egg, then bake for 8–10 minutes, until golden. Cool on a wire rack.

Slice a small 'lid' from the top of each cooled bun. Scoop out a bit of each bun centre and add it to a mixing bowl. To make the filling, add the 50ml of milk, along with the almond paste and almonds to the bowl and mix to a thick paste. Fill each bun with a spoonful of this mixture. To finish, pipe or spoon the whipped cream over the filling, then replace the 'lids' and dust with icing sugar to serve.

— **FRASVÅFFLOR PÅ TVÅ SÄTT** —

Swedish Waffles Two Ways

You'll need a Swedish waffle iron for these, but you'll find one easily online and it's so worth the investment (be sure to get a Swedish version, not the deeper kind). Light, crisp and heart-shaped, waffles are a *fika* favourite in Sweden – especially when we're skiing. Big or small, every resort has a waffle hut. There are two main ways to make them: the original way, which gives perfectly crispy results; and a second way, which is more complicated but yields the most amazingly crisp waffles I think you will ever eat.

MAKES 6–8

200g plain flour
1 teaspoon baking powder
1 tablespoon caster sugar
a pinch of salt
300ml whole milk
100ml sparkling water, chilled
75g butter, melted, plus more (melted) for brushing
1 teaspoon vanilla extract (optional)

The first way

Sift the flour and baking powder into a mixing bowl. Stir in the sugar and salt to combine. Make a well in the centre and, little by little, whisk in the milk. Once you've added all the milk, whisk in the sparkling water and melted butter, and the vanilla, if using.

Heat your waffle iron and brush it with a little more melted butter. Pour in the batter according to the manufacturer's instructions, and cook the waffles one by one, until golden and crisp.

Serve immediately with whipped cream, and berry compôte, fresh berries or lingonberry jam.

MAKES 8–10

180g plain flour
1 teaspoon baking powder
a pinch of salt
250ml double cream
50g butter, melted and cooled, plus more (melted) for brushing

TO SERVE (EITHER WAY)
lightly whipped cream
berry compôte, fresh berries or lingonberry jam

The second way

Sift the flour, baking powder and salt into a large mixing bowl. Little by little, add 250ml of cold water, whisking between each addition.

In a separate bowl, whip the cream until it forms soft peaks, then gently fold the whipped cream into the batter until no streaks remain. Stir in the butter.

Heat your waffle iron and brush it with a little more melted butter. Pour in the batter according to the manufacturer's instructions, and cook the waffles one by one, until golden and crisp.

Let the waffles cool slightly on a wire rack if you want to preserve the crispiness, then serve immediately with whipped cream, and berry compôte, fresh berries or lingonberry jam.

— **RABARBERPAJ MED VANILJSÅS** —

Rhubarb Pie with Vanilla Sauce

Rhubarb comes into season somewhere between May and early July – and that's when this pie becomes a staple at the family table. The filling is sharp and juicy, and the topping is more like a crisp than a classic pastry. The vanilla sauce, here served chilled (but is equally good warm), is almost as important as the pie itself – at least, that's the case in my family.

SERVES 6

100g caster sugar
1 tablespoon potato starch or cornflour
500g rhubarb, trimmed and chopped into 2cm pieces
150g plain flour
125g butter, diced and chilled
100g light brown soft sugar
a pinch of salt

FOR THE VANILLA SAUCE
300ml whole milk
1 teaspoon vanilla extract or ½ vanilla pod
2 egg yolks
1 tablespoon caster sugar

First, make the sauce. Pour the milk into a small saucepan and place it over a low–medium heat. Add the vanilla and heat gently until bubbles just appear at the edges of the milk, but it's not boiling. Remove the pan from the heat.

In a large bowl, whisk together the yolks and tablespoon of sugar until pale and combined. Whisking continuously, pour in the hot milk mixture (remove the vanilla pod, if necessary), until fully combined.

Pour the mixture back into a clean pan and place it over a medium–low heat. Gently stir the sauce until thickened enough to coat the back of a spoon (about 5 minutes – take care as it can quickly become too thick; keep an eye on it). Pour the sauce into a jug, leave it to cool, then cover and refrigerate until chilled.

While the sauce is chilling, make the pie. Heat the oven to 220°C/200°C fan.

Tip the sugar and potato starch or cornflour into a mixing bowl and stir to combine. Add the rhubarb and toss to coat the pieces evenly. Spoon the coated rhubarb into a 25cm-diameter baking dish (about 5cm deep) in an even layer and set aside.

In a mixing bowl, rub together the plain flour and butter until the mixture resembles coarse breadcrumbs. Stir in the brown sugar and salt. Scatter this over the rhubarb.

Place the pie in the oven to bake for 30–35 minutes, until the topping is golden and the rhubarb beneath is tender. Remove it from the oven and leave it to cool until warm. Serve the pie warm with the chilled vanilla sauce for pouring over.

— SPRÖDA KEX MED SMAK AV BLÅMÖGELOST OCH INGEFÄRA —

Blue Cheese and Ginger Biscuits

A surprising but addictive combination of creamy blue cheese and warm ginger spice, these savoury biscuits are perfect with wine, or with traditional Swedish *glögg* – a warm punch of spiced whiskey and rum.

MAKES ABOUT 35

150g butter, softened
100g blue cheese (such as Ädelost, Stilton or gorgonzola)
200g plain flour, plus more for rolling
½ teaspoon ground ginger
1 tablespoon finely chopped crystallised ginger (optional)
a pinch of salt

Cream the butter and cheese together in a bowl until smooth, then mix in the flour, ground ginger, crystallised ginger (if using) and salt until you have a soft dough. Shape the dough into a ball, wrap it in cling film and refrigerate for 1 hour to rest and firm up.

Once the dough has chilled, heat the oven to 200°C/180°C fan and line two baking sheets with baking paper.

While the oven is heating up, roll out the chilled dough on a lightly floured work surface to 6mm thick. Using a 5cm round cutter, stamp out rounds of the dough, re-rolling the trimmings just once so as not to overwork it. You should get about 35 rounds altogether.

Place the rounds on the lined baking sheets spacing them well apart. Bake for 10–12 minutes, until lightly golden, then transfer them to a wire rack to cool and firm up. The biscuits will keep in an airtight container for about 1 week.

— KARDEMUMMABULLAR —
Cardamom Buns

I'm closing the book with my favourite – cardamom buns (cinnamon buns are lovely, but for me, like many Swedes, it's the cardamom bun that really hits the spot). With its warm, spicy scent and smooth filling, these buns are an essential part of the *fika* table.

MAKES ABOUT 16

FOR THE DOUGH
250ml whole milk
25g fresh yeast or 7g instant dried yeast
45g caster sugar
1 teaspoon ground cardamom
½ teaspoon salt
400g plain flour (or use bread flour), plus more for rolling
75g butter, chopped, at room temperature

FOR THE FILLING
75g butter, at room temperature
65g caster sugar
1–1½ teaspoons ground cardamom, according to taste

TO FINISH
1 egg, beaten
15g unsalted butter, melted

Pour the milk into a saucepan over a low–medium heat and warm it until it reaches 37°C on a thermometer ('blood' temperature – lukewarm to the skin). Crumble the yeast into a mixing bowl or tip in the dried yeast, pour over the warm milk and stir to dissolve.

By hand, or in a stand mixer fitted with the dough hook on medium speed, add the sugar, cardamom and salt, stirring to combine. Little by little, add the flour, kneading between additions. Add the butter and knead for 8–10 minutes to a smooth, elastic and slightly shiny dough. Cover the bowl with a clean tea towel and let the dough rise in a warm place for about 45–60 minutes, until doubled in volume.

Meanwhile, make the filling by mixing together the butter, sugar and cardamom in a bowl until smooth and spreadable. Set aside. Grease two 23–25cm springform cake tins with butter.

Tip out the risen dough on to a lightly dusted work surface. Form it into a rectangle, then roll it out to a rectangle measuring 30cm × 40cm. Spread the filling evenly over the surface, to the edges. With a long side closest to you, pick up the edge of the dough and roll it on to the filling, as tightly as you can all along the length. Roll all the way to the opposite edge to create a log. Turn the log so that the seam is underneath. With a sharp knife, trim each end, discard the trimmings, then cut along the length to create 16 equal slices.

Turn the slices so that the spiral is facing upwards and position the buns to form a ring and a centre in each tin (gaps are fine – the buns will nudge together as they prove and bake). Cover each tin with a tea towel and leave the buns to prove at room temperature for 30 minutes while you heat the oven to 250°C/230°C fan.

Once the buns are puffy, brush each one with egg. Bake in the centre of the oven for 10–12 minutes, until risen and golden brown. Brush with the melted butter, leave to cool slightly in the tin, then release and gently tear them apart to serve warm. They will keep in an airtight container for up to 3 days – refresh in the oven to serve.

Index

A

aïoli, herb 140
almond paste: Swedish semlor 246
almonds: cucumber and sprouted almond salad with sumac 34
Finnish almond biscuits 241
fried kale with grated almond and garlic vinaigrette 98
soft almond cookies 232
anchovies: potato and Swedish anchovy gratin 137
Swedish anchovies 134
Swedish anchovy and potato salad 134
ångkokta blåmusslor med äpple och dragon 126
ansjovis 134
apples: boiled yellow wax beans with dill butter and apple 88
fried pork with onion sauce, corn and sliced apple 152
steamed mussels with apples and tarragon 126
Arctic char with spinach, broccoli, new potato and horseradish salad 120
artichokes see **Jerusalem artichokes**
ärtsoppa och pannkakor 39
asparagus: egg & courgette omelette 33
hollandaise sauce with boiled asparagus and cayenne pepper 91

B

bacon: blood pudding 172
baking 192–5
beef: biff rydberg with parsley and fried egg 183
fillet of beef with roasted root vegetables and crispy potato matchsticks 178
Swedish meatballs with potatoes, lingonberries and pressed cucumber 169–70
toast Pelle Janzon 180
beer: blood pudding 172

beetroot: baked beetroot with cucumber ribbons and crown dill 72
hot-smoked salmon salad with pickled beetroots, new potatoes and parsley 132
open sandwiches on rye bread 225
vegetable stew with potatoes, Romanesco, golden beetroots and Brussels sprouts 85
biff rydberg med persilja och stekt ägg 183
biff rydberg with parsley and fried egg 183
biscuits see **cookies**
blåbärsmuffins 205
blåbärssoppa med saffranskorpor och gräddvirvel 86
blodpudding 172
blomkålssoppa med rostade solroskärnor 70
blood pudding 172
blue cheese and ginger biscuits 254
blueberries: blueberry muffins 205
blueberry soup with saffron rusks 86
cabbage salad with blueberries 30
bread: croûtons 28
flatbread 216
homemade rye bread 226
open sandwiches on rye bread 225–6
Swedish flatbreads with Queen's jam and butter 211
toast Pelle Janzon 180
toast Skagen with fresh lemon 106
breadcrumbs: fried wallenbergare 184
Swedish meatballs 169–70
brine 160
broad beans with mint salad 62
broccoli: whole roasted Arctic char with spinach, broccoli, new potato and horseradish salad 120
Brussels sprouts: creamy game stew with Brussels sprouts,

sunflower seeds and kohlrabi salad 188
vegetable stew with potatoes, Romanesco, golden beetroots and Brussels sprouts 85
buns: cardamom buns 192, 257
cinnamon buns 192, 197–8
saffron buns 219–20
Swedish semlor 246
vanilla buns 199–200
butter: clarifying 40
dill butter 88
grilled pointed cabbage with lemon butter 44
hollandaise sauce 91
buttermilk: homemade rye bread 226

C

cabbage: cabbage pudding with kale and lingonberries 176
cabbage salad with blueberries 30
grilled pointed cabbage with lemon butter 44
grilled pork with creamy pointed cabbage 167
quick cabbage rolls 155
see also red cabbage
cakes: carrot cake with lemon frosting 234
Swedish chocolate cake 244
capers: cubed new potatoes fried in clarified butter with capers and dill 40
Danish remoulade 130
shredded red cabbage salad with capers and lemon zest 36
caramel: caramel cookies 228
plum tarte tatin 208
cardamom: cardamom buns 192, 257
Swedish semlor 246
carrots: carrot cake with lemon frosting 234
slow-cooked pork shank with mashed root vegetables and watercress 160

Index

whole roasted flatfish with oven-baked potatoes, carrots and garlic 130
cauliflower: cauliflower soup with roasted sunflower seeds 70
salad 186
vegetable stew with potatoes, Romanesco, golden beetroots and Brussels sprouts 85
cayenne pepper: hollandaise sauce with boiled asparagus and cayenne pepper 91
celeriac: fillet of beef with roasted root vegetables 178
char: whole roasted Arctic char with spinach, broccoli, new potato and horseradish salad 120
cheese: blue cheese and ginger biscuits 254
cabbage salad with blueberries and shaved frozen feta 30
fish and cheesy béchamel gratin in a potato crown 129
honey and basil marinated strawberries with frozen feta 80
open sandwiches on rye bread 225
Swedish cheese pie 222
chia seeds: seed crispbread 242
chicken liver pâté 150
open sandwiches on rye bread 226
chocolate: chocolate balls 214
chocolate slices 236
Swedish chocolate cake 244
chokladbollar 214
chokladsnittar 236
cinnamon buns 192, 197–8
clarifying butter 40
cod: pan-fried cod with mashed potatoes, egg sauce and red onion 116
coffee: chocolate balls 214
Cognac: chicken liver pâté 150
cookies and biscuits: blue cheese and ginger biscuits 254
caramel cookies 228
chocolate slices 236
Finnish almond biscuits 241
raspberry dreams 231
soft almond cookies 232
cottage cheese: open sandwiches on rye bread 225
courgettes: egg & courgette omelette 33
marinated courgettes with flowers and mint 66
salad with raspberries, courgettes and chives 58
crackers: seed crispbread 242
cream: blueberry soup 86
fried mushrooms with peas and burnt cream 64
potato pancakes with lingonberries and soured cream 61
Swedish semlor 246
Swedish waffles 249
vanilla buns 199–200
cream cheese: lemon frosting 234
crème fraîche: creamy potato salad with kale, cucumber and radishes 48
smoked fish with soft-boiled egg, pickled red onion and flatbread 125
croûtons 28
cucumber: baked beetroot with cucumber ribbons and crown dill 72
creamy potato salad with kale, cucumber and radishes 48
cucumber and sprouted almond salad with sumac 34
open sandwiches on rye bread 226
Swedish meatballs with potatoes, lingonberries and pressed cucumber 169–70
cured salmon 110
curry: Danish remoulade 130
custard: saffron buns 219–20

D

Danish remoulade 130
dill: baked beetroot with cucumber ribbons and crown dill 72
cubed new potatoes fried in clarified butter with capers and dill 40
cured salmon 110
dill butter 88
fennel and orange salad with dill 52
mustard dill sauce 114
Romaine salad with dill and croûtons 28
dumplings: Swedish dumplings with meat filling 163

E

eggs: biff rydberg with parsley and fried egg 183
egg & courgette omelette 33
gravad lax with poached egg and mustard dill sauce 114
open sandwiches on rye bread 226
pan-fried cod with mashed potatoes, egg sauce and red onion 116
salmon pudding 142
smoked fish with soft-boiled egg, pickled red onion and flatbread 125
toast Pelle Janzon 180

F

fänkåls- och apelsinsallad med dill och tranbär 52
fennel: fennel and orange salad with dill 52
fish soup with saffron and fennel 140
fika 192–5
Finnish almond biscuits 241
finska pinnar 241
fish 103–4
fish and cheesy béchamel gratin in a potato crown 129
fish soup with saffron and fennel 140
whole roasted flatfish with oven-baked potatoes, carrots and garlic 130
see also **cod**, **herring**, **salmon** *etc*
fisksoppa med saffran och fänkål 140
flatbreads 216
Swedish flatbreads with Queen's jam and butter 211
flax seeds: homemade rye bread 226
seed crispbread 242

frasvåfflor på två sätt 249
fröknäcke 242
frosting, lemon 234
fyra sorters smörrebröd och ett hembakat rågbröd 225

G

game stew with Brussels sprouts, sunflower seeds and kohlrabi salad 188
garlic: grated almond and garlic vinaigrette 98
  herb aïoli 140
  whole roasted flatfish with oven-baked potatoes, carrots and garlic 130
gherkins: Danish remoulade 130
ginger: blue cheese and ginger biscuits 254
gratins: fish and cheesy béchamel gratin in a potato crown 129
  potato and Swedish anchovy gratin 137
gravad lax 110
gravad lax med pocherat ägg och hovmästarsås 114
gravad lax with poached egg and mustard dill sauce 114
green beans: broad beans with mint salad 62
grillad kålrabbi 51
grillad spetskål med citronsmör 44
grillade fläskkotletter med krämig spetskål 167
gubbröra 134
gurksallad med groddad sötmandel och sumak 34

H

hallongrottor 231
hasselback potatoes with fried venison fillet and mushroom compôte 186
hjortfilé med hasselbackspotatis och stekt svamp 186
hazelnuts: cinnamon buns with hazelnuts 197–8
  hazelnut and parsley pesto 92
helgrillad kålrot med salvia 54
helstekt plattfisk med rostade rotfrukter och vitlök 130
helstekt röding med färskpotatis och mycket grönt 120
herb aïoli 140
herb oil 178
herring: open sandwiches on rye bread 226
  pickled fried herring with red onion and rye bread 'Tore Wretman-style' 109
hollandaise sauce with boiled asparagus and cayenne pepper 91
honey and basil marinated strawberries with frozen feta 80
horseradish: fried wallenbergare with peas, horseradish and lemon 184
  whole roasted Arctic char with spinach, broccoli, new potato and horseradish salad 120

J

jam: raspberry dreams 231
Janssons frestelse 137
Janzon, Pelle 180
Jerusalem artichoke soup with herbs 96
jordärtskockssoppa med färska örter 96

K

kale: cabbage pudding with kale and lingonberries 176
  creamy potato salad with kale, cucumber and radishes 48
  fried kale with grated almond and garlic vinaigrette 98
kålpudding med grönkål och lingon 176
kanelbulle med hasselnötsfyllning 197–8
kardemummabullar 257
kladdkaka 244
klassisk fiskgratäng med dill och räkor 129
klassisk grönsakssoppa med potatis 85
kohlrabi: creamy game stew with Brussels sprouts, sunflower seeds and kohlrabi salad 188
  grilled kohlrabi 51
kokta vaxbönor med dillsmör och äpple 88
kolakakor 228
köttbullar med potatis, lingon och inlagd gurka 169–70
krämig potatissallad med grönkål, gurka och rädisor 48
kroppkakor 163
kycklingleverpastej 150

L

lagom 147
långkokt fläsklägg med rotmos 160
laxpudding 142
leeks: fish soup with saffron and fennel 140
lemon: carrot cake with lemon frosting 234
  grilled pointed cabbage with lemon butter 44
  shredded red cabbage salad with capers and lemon zest 36
  toast Skagen with fresh lemon 106
lettuce: Romaine salad with dill and croûtons 28
  salad 186
lingonberries: cabbage pudding with kale and lingonberries 176
  potato pancakes with lingonberries and soured cream 61
liver: chicken liver pâté 150

M

mackerel see **smoked mackerel**
mjuka mandelkakor 232
marinerad zucchini med blommor och mynta 66
mayonnaise: Danish remoulade 130
  herb aïoli 140
  smoked fish with soft-boiled egg, pickled red onion and flatbread 125
  toast Skagen with fresh lemon 106

Index

meat 147
   cabbage pudding with kale and lingonberries 176
   see also **beef**, **pork** *etc*
meatballs 147
   Swedish meatballs with potatoes, lingonberries and pressed cucumber 169–70
milk: vanilla sauce 252
mint salad, broad beans with 62
morotskaka med citronfrosting 234
muffins, blueberry 205
mushrooms: creamy game stew with Brussels sprouts, sunflower seeds and kohlrabi salad 188
   fried mushrooms with peas and burnt cream 64
   hasselback potatoes with fried venison fillet and mushroom compôte 186
   open sandwiches on rye bread 225
mussels: steamed mussels with apples and tarragon 126
mustard dill sauce 114

O

oats: chocolate balls 214
oil, herb 178
omelette, egg & courgette 33
onions: biff rydberg with parsley and fried egg 183
   fried pork with onion sauce, corn and sliced apple 152
   pan-fried cod with mashed potatoes, egg sauce and red onion 116
   pickled fried herring with red onion and rye bread 'Tore Wretman-style' 109
   pickled red onion 125
   potato and Swedish anchovy gratin 137
open sandwiches on rye bread 225–6
oranges: fennel and orange salad with dill 52
oxfilé med rostade rotfrukter och tändstickspotatis 178

P

pancakes: pancakes with lingonberry jam and cream 39
   potato pancakes with lingonberries and soured cream 61
   thick pancake 238
parsley: biff rydberg with parsley and fried egg 183
   hazelnut and parsley pesto 92
   herb oil 178
   hot-smoked salmon salad with pickled beetroots, new potatoes and parsley 132
   parsley and thyme salad 64
   tomato and parsley salad 33
pastry 222
pâtés: chicken liver pâté 150
   open sandwiches on rye bread 226
patties: fried wallenbergare 184
pears: sautéed spinach with pears and pork chops 158
peas: fried mushrooms with peas and burnt cream 64
   fried wallenbergare with peas, horseradish and lemon 184
   split pea soup with pork 39
   whole roasted Arctic char with spinach, broccoli, new potato and horseradish salad 120
pesto, hazelnut and parsley 92
pickles: pickled fried herring 109
   pickled red onion 125
   pressed cucumber 169–70
pies: rhubarb pie with vanilla sauce 252
   Swedish cheese pie 222
pig's blood: blood pudding 172
'pizza salad' 30
plum tarte tatin 208
pork: fried pork with onion sauce, corn and sliced apple 152
   grilled pork with creamy pointed cabbage 167
   quick cabbage rolls 155
   sautéed spinach with pears and pork chops 158
   slow-cooked pork shank with mashed root vegetables and watercress 160
   split pea soup with pork 39
   Swedish dumplings with meat filling 163
   Swedish meatballs with potatoes, lingonberries and pressed cucumber 169–70
potatoes: biff rydberg with parsley and fried egg 183
   creamy potato salad with kale, cucumber and radishes 48
   crispy potato matchsticks 178
   cubed new potatoes fried in clarified butter with capers and dill 40
   fillet of beef with roasted root vegetables and crispy potato matchsticks 178
   fish and cheesy béchamel gratin in a potato crown 129
   hasselback potatoes with fried venison fillet and mushroom compôte 186
   hot-smoked salmon salad with pickled beetroots, new potatoes and parsley 132
   pan-fried cod with mashed potatoes, egg sauce and red onion 116
   potato and Swedish anchovy gratin 137
   potato pancakes with lingonberries and soured cream 61
   salmon pudding 142
   slow-cooked pork shank with mashed root vegetables and watercress 160
   Swedish anchovy and potato salad 134
   Swedish dumplings with meat filling 163
   Swedish meatballs with potatoes, lingonberries and pressed cucumber 169–70
   vegetable stew with potatoes, Romanesco, golden beetroots and Brussels sprouts 85
   whole roasted Arctic char with spinach, broccoli, new potato and horseradish salad 120
   whole roasted flatfish with oven-baked potatoes, carrots and garlic 130
prawns: fish and cheesy béchamel gratin in a potato crown 129

fish soup with saffron and fennel 140
toast Skagen with fresh lemon 106
pumpa-och saffranssufflé 77
pumpkin: pumpkin and saffron soufflé 77
roasted pumpkin purée 78
pumpkin seeds: homemade rye bread 226
seed crispbread 242

Q

quark: saffron buns 219–20

R

rabarberkompott med yoghurt 69
rabarberpaj med vaniljsås 252
radishes: creamy potato salad with kale, cucumber and radishes 48
open sandwiches on rye bread 225
raggmunk med lingon och gräddfil 61
raspberries: salad with raspberries, courgettes and chives 58
raspberry jam: raspberry dreams 231
red cabbage salad with capers and lemon zest 36
remoulade, Danish 130
rhubarb: rhubarb compôte with yoghurt 69
rhubarb pie with vanilla sauce 252
rice: cabbage pudding with kale and lingonberries 176
quick cabbage rolls 155
rödkålssallad med kapris och citronskal 36
roe: toast Pelle Janzon 180
rökt fisk med ägg, picklad rödlök och riven pepparrot 125
Romaine salad with dill and croûtons 28
Romanesco cauliflower: vegetable stew with potatoes, Romanesco, golden beetroots and Brussels sprouts 85

romansallat med dill och krutonger 28
root vegetables: fillet of beef with roasted root vegetables 178
slow-cooked pork shank with mashed root vegetables and watercress 160
rutabaga *see* **swede**
rye bread, open sandwiches on 225–6
rye flour: blood pudding 172
flatbread 216
homemade rye bread 226
pickled fried herring with red onion and rye bread 'Tore Wretman-style' 109

S

saffransbullar 219–20
saffron: fish soup with saffron and fennel 140
pumpkin and saffron soufflé 77
saffron buns 219–20
salads 186
broad beans with mint salad 62
cabbage salad with blueberries 30
creamy potato salad with kale, cucumber and radishes 48
cucumber and sprouted almond salad with sumac 34
fennel and orange salad with dill 52
hot-smoked salmon salad with pickled beetroots, new potatoes and parsley 132
parsley and thyme salad 64
Romaine salad with dill and croûtons 28
salad with raspberries, courgettes and chives 58
shredded red cabbage salad with capers and lemon zest 36
spinach, broccoli, new potatoes and horseradish salad 120
Swedish anchovy and potato salad 134
tomato and parsley salad 33
sallad med bönor, linser och mynta 62
sallad med hallon, zucchini och

rädisor 58
salmon: cured salmon 110
gravad lax with poached egg and mustard dill sauce 114
salmon pudding 142
see also **smoked salmon**
salsify with hazelnut and parsley pesto 92
salt: brine 160
cured salmon 110
salted pork: fried pork with onion sauce, corn and sliced apple 152
slow-cooked pork shank with mashed root vegetables and watercress 160
sandwiches: open sandwiches on rye bread 225–6
sauces: hazelnut and parsley pesto 92
hollandaise sauce 91
mustard dill sauce 114
vanilla sauce 252
seed crispbread 242
sesame seeds: seed crispbread 242
semlor 246
smoked mackerel: smoked fish with soft-boiled egg, pickled red onion and flatbread 125
smoked salmon: hot-smoked salmon salad with pickled beetroots, new potatoes and parsley 132
smörstekt potatis med kapris och dill 40
snabba kåldolmar 155
soft almond cookies 232
söta jordgubbar med basilika och fryst fetaost 80
soufflé, pumpkin and saffron 77
soups: blueberry soup with saffron rusks 86
cauliflower soup with roasted sunflower seeds 70
fish soup with saffron and fennel 140
Jerusalem artichoke soup with herbs 96
split pea soup with pork 39
soured cream, potato pancakes with lingonberries and 61
sparris med hollandaisesås och cayennepeppar 91

spinach: sautéed spinach with pears and pork chops 158
smoked fish with soft-boiled egg, pickled red onion and flatbread 125
whole roasted Arctic char with spinach, broccoli, new potato and horseradish salad 120
split pea soup with pork 39
spröda kex med smak av blåmögelost och ingefära 254
stekt fläsk med löksås, majs och skivat äpple 152
stekt grönkål med mandel- och vitlöksvinägrett 98
stekt inlagd strömming på Tore Wretmans vis 109
stekt svamp med gröna ärter och bränd grädde 64
stekta kotletter med sauterad spenat och päron 158
stews: creamy game stew 188
vegetable stew 85
strawberries: honey and basil marinated strawberries with frozen feta 80
rhubarb compôte with yoghurt 69
sunflower seeds: cauliflower soup with roasted sunflower seeds 70
creamy game stew with Brussels sprouts, sunflower seeds and kohlrabi salad 188
homemade rye bread 226
seed crispbread 242
svartrötter med hasselnöts- och persiljepesto 92
swede: slow-cooked pork shank with mashed root vegetables and watercress 160
whole roasted swede with sage 54
Swedish anchovies 134
potato and Swedish anchovy gratin 137
Swedish anchovy and potato salad 134
Swedish cheese pie 222
Swedish chocolate cake 244
Swedish dumplings with meat filling 163
Swedish flatbreads with Queen's jam and butter 211
Swedish meatballs with potatoes, lingonberries and pressed cucumber 169–70
Swedish semlor 246
Swedish waffles 249
sweetcorn: fried pork with onion sauce, corn and sliced apple 152

T

tarragon, steamed mussels with apples and 126
tarts: plum tarte tatin 208
Swedish cheese pie 222
tarte tatin med plommon 208
tekakor med smör och drottningsylt 211
thick pancake 238
thyme: parsley and thyme salad 64
toast Pelle Janzon 180
toast Skagen with fresh lemon 106
tomato and parsley salad 33
torsk med pressad potatis, äggsås och rödlök 116
tunnbröd 216

U

ugnspannkaka 238
ugnsrostade rödbetor med gurka och krondill 72

V

vaniljbullar 199–200
vanilla: vanilla buns 199–200
vanilla sauce 252
varmrökt lax med potatissallad och inlagda rödbetor 132
västerbottenspaj 222
veal: fried wallenbergare with peas, horseradish and lemon 184
Swedish meatballs with potatoes, lingonberries and pressed cucumber 169–70
vegetables 25–6
vegetable stew 85
see also **beetroot**, **potatoes** *etc*
vendace roe: toast Pelle Janzon 180
venison: hasselback potatoes with fried venison fillet and mushroom compôte 186
viltgryta med brysselkål och kålrabbisallad 188
vinaigrette, grated almond and garlic 98
vitkålsallad med blåbär och fryst fetaost 30

W

waffles, Swedish 249
wallenbergare med gröna ärter, pepparrot och citron 184
watercress, slow-cooked pork shank with mashed root vegetables and 160
wine: fish soup with saffron and fennel 140
steamed mussels with apples and tarragon 126
Wretman, Tore 109, 147, 169

Y

yeast: cardamom buns 257
cinnamon buns with hazelnuts 197–8
flatbread 216
saffron buns 219–20
Swedish flatbreads with Queen's jam and butter 211
Swedish semlor 246
vanilla buns 199–200
yellow wax beans with dill butter and apple 88
yoghurt, rhubarb compôte with 69

Z

zucchiniomelett med tomat- och persiljesallad 33

Thank You

This book wouldn't be possible without many people. Thank you to the team at Bloomsbury for their support and encouragement: Rowan Yapp, Jon Croft, Emily North, Isobel Turton and Rob Cox. And to Jude Barratt for her incredible eagle eyes in the editing, and Caroline Stearns for Americanizing the book for the US edition.

Thank you to the shoot team, who came to Stockholm and beautifully captured my food and made it shine: Liz Haarala and Max Hamilton, and Jen Kay for the gorgeous props.

Thanks to Peter Moffat for bringing it all together in a beautiful design.

And finally, thank you to my family – none of this would be possible without you.

About the Author

Niklas Ekstedt is a Michelin-star chef, restaurateur and presenter. He opened his first two restaurants in his early twenties and was soon hosting his first cooking show *Mat* ('food' in Swedish) on Swedish national television. Before long, Niklas was drawn back to his Scandinavian roots as he spent a summer experimenting with traditional methods of cooking over fire – and from here, there was no going back.

In 2011, he opened Ekstedt in Stockholm, where traditional techniques meet bold creativity and every dish is cooked over open flames. The restaurant was awarded a Michelin star in 2013 and has held one ever since. Niklas opened his first international outpost, Ekstedt at The Yard, in London in 2021 to great critical acclaim.

Niklas has appeared on UK TV screens as a regular guest on *Saturday Kitchen*, *MasterChef* and the Channel 4 series *Crazy Delicious*. Niklas has authored several cookbooks in his mission to continue to explore age-old techniques and to share the lost art of cooking with chefs and home cooks alike. *The Swedish Cookbook* is his fifth book.

BLOOMSBURY PUBLISHING
Bloomsbury Publishing Plc
50 Bedford Square, London, WC1B 3DP, UK
Bloomsbury Publishing Ireland Limited,
29 Earlsfort Terrace, Dublin 2, D02 AY28, Ireland

BLOOMSBURY, BLOOMSBURY PUBLISHING and the Diana logo
are trademarks of Bloomsbury Publishing Plc

First published in Great Britain, 2026

Text © Niklas Ekstedt, 2026
Photographs © Haarala Hamilton, 2026
Cover illustration © Jonna Fransson, 2026

Niklas Ekstedt and Elizabeth Haarala and Max Hamilton have asserted their right
under the Copyright, Designs and Patents Act, 1988, to be identified as author
and photographers, respectively, of this work

All rights reserved. No part of this publication may be: i) reproduced or transmitted in
any form, electronic or mechanical, including photocopying, recording or by means
of any information storage or retrieval system without prior permission in writing from
the publishers; or ii) used or reproduced in any way for the training, development or
operation of artificial intelligence (AI) technologies, including generative AI technologies.
The rights holders expressly reserve this publication from the text and data mining
exception as per Article 4(3) of the Digital Single Market Directive (EU) 2019/790

A catalogue record for this book is available from the British Library

ISBN: HB: 978-1-5266-7970-3; eBook: 978-1-5266-7971-0

2 4 6 8 10 9 7 5 3 1

Editorial Director: Rowan Yapp
Project Editor: Emily North
Editor: Judy Barratt
Designer: Peter Moffat at Jon Croft Editions
Photographer: Haarala Hamilton
Prop Stylist: Jen Kay
Production: Laura Brodie

Printed and bound in China by C&C Offset Printing Co., Ltd.

To find out more about our authors and books
visit www.bloomsbury.com and sign up for our newsletters

For product safety related questions contact productsafety@bloomsbury.com